Snow and Ice Climbing

Snow and Ice Climbing

JOHN BARRY

CLOUDCAP
SEATTLE

First published in Great Britain in 1987 by
The Crowood Press

**Published in North America by Cloudcap
Box 27344, Seattle, Washington 98125**

This edition not for sale outside the USA and Canada

ISBN 0-938567-02-0

**For my boys, Joseph and John-Mark: but only in case
they can find no better diversion.**

'Speak as they please what does the mountain care?
Ah, but a man's reach should exceed his grasp,
Or what's a heaven for?'
                                Robert Browning

Acknowledgements

Thanks to Nigel Shepherd, Malcolm Campbell, John Cousins,
Mick Woolridge and Rob Collister and a dozen other winter
climbing partners for advice, criticism and assistance of one
kind or another. Thanks also to Sarah Bishop for the diagrams;
Jim Curran and Lesley Campbell for assistance with the black
and white photography; Dave Nicholls for that very first ice
climb way back; Climber & Rambler Outdoor Equipment,
Betws-y-Coed and Joe Brown's of Capel Curig who kindly
allowed me to photograph their wares; James A. Wilkerson
MD; and Kath and Fiona for typing at double any mortal rate.

Typeset by Action Typesetting Ltd, Gloucester
Printed and bound in Great Britain by
BPCC Hazell Books, Aylesbury

Contents

Introduction

I doubt if anyone knows exactly when man first took up his axe and used it to climb. I have read that in 1812 Colome Hawker cut steps in ice on Ben Lomond, in which case he may have started it all – started a great snow and ice climbing game that has been played, full tilt and almost continuously, somewhere on this earth ever since. Nowhere is it played more enthusiastically than in the British Isles; in Scotland in particular, but in England and Wales too, given a half decent, that is a sufficiently cold, winter. On a few hundred feet of 40-degree snow, on several thousand feet of near vertical ice, or on anything and everything in between you'll find the players of the game hard at it with the first hint of frost or snowfall; in teams of one, two, three and upward, playing up, playing hard and trying to get their 'retaliation in first' while they are:

'Scrambling, slipping,
Pulling, pushing,
Lifting, gasping,
Looking, hoping,
Despairing, climbing,
Holding on, falling off,
Trying, puffing,
Loosing, gathering,
Talking, stepping,
Grumbling, anathematising,
Scraping, hacking,
Bumping, jogging,
Overturning, hunting,
Straddling – for know you that by these

methods alone are the most divine mysteries of the Quest reached.'
'Divine Mysteries of the Oromaniacal Quest', Norman Collie, *Scottish Mountaineering Club Journal,* 1894.

In truth it is a game of esoteric pleasures. Whilst this book is primarily concerned with climbing on snow and ice in Britain, most, if not all, of the skills and techniques described will work as well anywhere in the world; ice is ice and snow snow, from the Ben, to the Baltoro, to beyond.

Like most of the other pursuits in the mountaineering family, snow and ice has suffered a change or two in code and practice over the years, and especially in the last ten years. Some have described this change as a revolution and it may be that 'suffered' should read 'benefited from'. No matter whether the change took place in the minds of men or in the equipment they use, or whether it was a bit of both – which it probably was – the happy fact is that the game is still played with as much gusto as ever it was. Since gusto is the vital ingredient, there's not much wrong with the current state of play.

This is a book for those who have had enough experience of rock climbing to know that they want more of the mountaineering game, but who as yet know nothing or little of climbing on snow and ice; for those who would like to know something or more and have gusto to add to learning and experience.

1 Equipment

BOOTS

'We-can-stick-out-'unger-thirst, an'
  weariness,
But-not-not-not-not the chronic sight of
  'em-
Boots-boots-boots-boots-movin' up an'
  down again!'
             'Boots', Rudyard Kipling

Climbing snow and ice demands a fairly
specialist kind of boot. Fortunately the same
boot can usually be used for mountaineering
in the Alps and other ranges (Scotland, Alps,
then wider ranges being the tiro's usual
progression) so the initial outlay is a better
investment than it might at first appear.
There is little to choose between most of the
'mountain' boots to be found in the shops
today. They commonly display the same
features: stiffened sole (essential on steep
ground); padded ankles and heels; fairly
high ankles (for support of ankles and
calves); hook and eye lacing; and some

Fig 1   A pair of trusty winter boots.

insulation. If all other things are equal, go for the most comfortable – you'll be spending long days in those boots.

The one difficult choice you will almost certainly have to make is leather or plastic. This is largely a matter of opinion. After that it's probably a matter of pocket. I hope that not too many experts will object if I say that, a faint come-back notwithstanding, plastic boots have all but ousted leather in the snow and ice game. There are good reasons: they are generally, if not universally, cheaper, lighter, quicker drying, more rigid of sole, and more accommodating of crampons (most plastic boots have pronounced flanges at heel and toe that eagerly accept cable and step-in bindings). They are also warmer – a big bonus – as they are always 'double boots', and, moreover, you will often have a choice of inners varying from cheap and warm to dear and hot. The strongest argument for leather boots is that they give a better feel, particularly on mixed ground. I grant them their case – and still prefer leather for summer alps – but the argument for plastic seems the stronger, especially for pure snow and ice, where 'feel' is less important than it is on rock, and particularly in Britain, where the wet and cold climate may mean the choice between wet leather-clad feet and dry plastic-clad feet.

Perhaps, having highlighted the advantages of plastic in boots, it is only fair to reveal what their detractors would say are their disadvantages. They are clumsy. This is true to a point. Get the smallest pair that is big enough and don't expect to dance like Fred Astaire. They are hard to wear in – true too. If they aren't comfortable in the shop they probably never will be, as plastic doesn't stretch easily, if at all. Some shops, certainly those that specialise in skiing boots, will have a heating and stretching device (in an effort to persuade buyers of those ski boots that their winter holiday week will not necessarily be as excruciating as their ten minutes' stomping round the shop floor in a giant pair of 'Franz Klammers'). If your plastic climbing boots were comfortable for the ten minutes you wore them in the shop, but aren't for the first ten minutes (or ten hours) on the hill, don't despair entirely. Seek out a shop with a ski boot stretcher, or take a knife to offending ankle flaps (with conservative care). Crippled by plastic recently on K2, I returned to the ranks of the walking wounded by removing square feet of the offending and unnecessary material from inside the ankles of the shell with a Swiss army knife.

Most people, certainly those with unremarkable feet, will find a make of plastic boots that is as comfortable as all but the oldest of leather boots. There are those who claim that, unlike leather, the very beauty of plastic boots is that they do not have to be worn in, as long as they fit correctly in the beginning, which only goes to show how contrary we so-called experts are! The most common models are by Koflach, Scarpa, Asolo, Brixia, Raichle, and Trezata. These days leather boots may be hard to come by, but the 'Super RD' by Galibier was a popular model that took some beating. Retailers are getting better at giving sound, experience-based advice, so make them earn their mark-up. Solicit guidance from climbers more experienced than yourself – they are seldom reluctant to part with their opinions.

Fig 2   A selection of good boots (from left to right): Vango Trezeta (plastic); Asolo AFS 101 (carbon fibre); Koflach Ultra (plastic); Leroux 'le phoque' – an interesting lightweight double boot, no longer available, but a very good boot should you ever chance to acquire a pair; Asolo '8000', a superb double boot with leather outer and neoprene inner; Dynafit 'Tourlite', a ski-mountaineering boot shown only because it is possible to climb ice in them which may be the most convenient solution if you have skied to your route; Yeti Supergaiters by Berghaus, a near perfect solution to the wet walk in – and a warm one too.

CRAMPONS

'Front-points are an extension of the mind.'
Instructional drivel

Oscar Eckenstein is generally credited with having invented the 10-point crampon in 1908. Since that day the features representing progress, apart from metallurgical advances, that have left us with lighter, stronger crampons, are:

1. The addition of two forward protruding points (the lobster claws of the 12-point crampon invented by Laurent Grivel in 1932).
2. A steady improvement in the means of fastening. I anticipate that all straps will soon be replaced by cable clip-ons, or 'step-ins' which are not unlike some ski bindings.
3. Greater ease of adjustment in width and length.

4. A choice of a rigid or articulated crampon (and, in some cases, that choice on the same crampon).

Most stores will stock over half a dozen different kinds of 12-point crampon, which, with their close relatives such as Footfangs, are the only serious suitors for the ice climber's foot. You will be faced with an initial choice of 'rigid' or 'articulated' (except in the case of Grivel F2s which ingeniously offer that choice on the same crampon). Rigid crampons, Footfangs included, are designed for climbing solely on ice (Footfangs for water-ice, on which they are incomparable), but unless you intend to devote your energies exclusively to that substance – and there's more fun to be had elsewhere – I'd advise against a rigid crampon. In any case, modern plastic boots are themselves so stiff that they render rigidity in a crampon almost redundant. Rigid crampons, being subject to greater stresses than their flexible counterparts, break more frequently. They also ball-up more readily and do not perform so well on mixed ground – that is, a mixture of rock, snow and ice – which is fairly common in the British Isles and in the Alps. However, since there is at least one model now available that converts from rigid to articulated in seconds, it may soon be that no choice has to

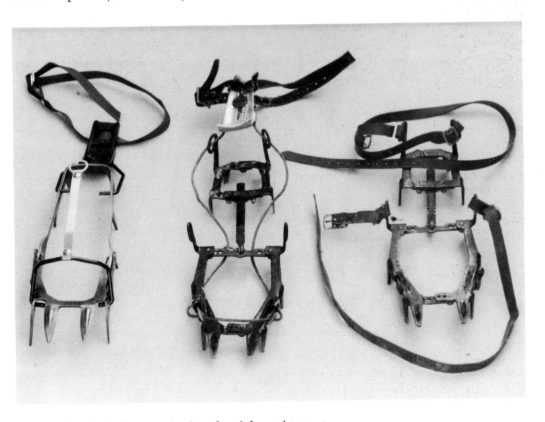

Fig 3   Three kinds of crampon binding (from left to right): step-in (Grivel F2); cable (Salewa Everest); strap-on (Salewa Everest).

be made. For the moment, if choice must be made, go for a hinged or articulated model.

You may be confronted with a further choice: there are two ways of arranging the front-points. These may be called 'standard' and 'French' front-points, since the second arrangement occurs most commonly on crampons of French design and manufacture. In use, the difference may be summarised thus: 'standard' front-points work well on every kind of terrain; 'French' front-points work *particularly* well on névé and on ice, but rather badly on mixed ground. This is because the lower pair of points bend to deny the upper ones free access to the rock.

The decision should be a fairly simple one: if you intend to climb on all manner of terrain and can afford only one pair of crampons, choose front-points of standard design. If, however, you intend to disport yourself exclusively on snow and ice, you will do well to invest in crampons with French front-points. If money is no object, you can own both and the world is your oyster. Grivel give a choice of front-points on their F2 model but it is one or the other – they are not interchangeable on the same crampon.

There is one other yet more specialist front-point – and it *is* singular, a single

Fig 4   Standard (left) and French (right) front-points.

proboscis-like front-point to each crampon. Such a system is unique to crampons made by Charlet-Moser. I have never climbed in them but am reliably informed that the hottest French cold climbers positively shin up frozen waterfalls wearing them. Be advised, though – they are for water-ice only.

The most common makers of 12-point crampons are Salewa, Grivel, Chouinard, SMC, Inter Alp, Laprade, Cassin, Stubai, and Charlet-Moser. Footfangs, made by Lowe, work on all terrain, like other crampons, but were designed specifically for steep water-ice on which surface they per-form best, and where they arguably out-perform traditional 12-pointers. Some Footfang fans claim that they are at least as good as any other crampon on any other terrain. I am not convinced.

Fit and Fastening

Major considerations in the selection of crampons are weight (the lighter the better), fit, and security of fastening. Fit and security are crucial and worth a careful look. If your crampons come off, the chances are that you will too. With good boots, however, and with correctly fitted, properly attached

Fig 5 Two tried and trusty articulated crampons: Salewa Classic (left), in four sizes, adjustable in length; Salewa Everest (right) adjustable in length and width.

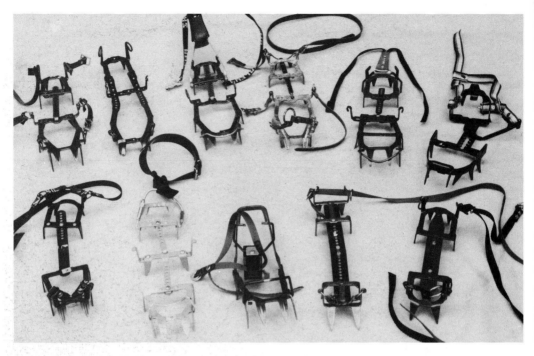

Fig 6   *A selection of modern crampons (top row, left to right): Salewa Hard Ice Classic; Salewa Chouinard Rigid; Salewa Messner Scissor (step-in); Salewa Adjustable Classic; Stubai Tirol (step-in); Stubai Ultra Perm; (bottom row, left to right) Cassin Flexible Ski Mountaineering Crampon; Camp K2 (step-in); Grivel F2 (step-in); Grivel Mountaineering Crampon; Stubai Ski Mountaineering Crampon.*

crampons, that is an easily avoided embarrassment.

Conventional teaching says that crampons ought to spring-fit the boots – that they should stay on a shaken boot without straps. I would argue that a fraction less than a spring-fit is the ideal. If your crampon fits your boot snugly when tinkering at home, the chances are that it will be too snug, infuriatingly snug, in some wild and spindrift-swept gully, which is the sort of place you'll end up putting them on. So a good fit, but a slack spring, perhaps. Some kinds of crampon have a wire heel-bar. If this is the case, ensure that the bar fits along the welt at the heel of the boot. Whilst a heel-bar is not essential, such an

arrangement does afford greater security. Some models of plastic boot have deep heels and you may need to replace the heel-bar with a longer piece of wire in order to locate it in the heel welt. This can be done easily at home with nothing more than a pair of pliers. It may take an hour of juggling with adjustments in length and width before you achieve a satisfactory fit, but once completed they should need no further alteration, unless, as sometimes happens, that good fit deteriorates into something sloppier at their first battering. In that case, a second look that night, with some minor tampering and those crampons should fit your boots for ever, though new boots are likely to mean new adjustments. When correctly fitted,

Fig 7   Salewa Everest with Chouinard neoprene straps on Asolo
'8000' boots. Note the arrangement of straps at the toe and the double
loop around the ankle.

(a)   (b)

Fig 8   Two views of Salewa Messner 'Scissors' with step-in bindings
on Asolo AFS 101 boots.

Fig 9   Grivel F2s on Koflach Ultra boots.

The method of passing the straps through the forward rings merits attention. The straps are locked by passing them through from the outside *on both posts*. This system also prevents the section of the strap that passes over the toes from sliding forward off the toe – and possibly off the boot (*see Fig 11*). A faster but equally secure system, which avoids the threading of the front rings, is to join the two front rings with a separate strap, or two shorter straps joined by a ring, through which the remaining foot strap is passed (*see Figs 12 and 14*). The Scots call this variation 'French rings' and the Americans call them 'Scots rings'! By whatever name, the length of the joined front straps is critical. If the loop formed by connecting the straps with a ring is too long it will be pulled, when tightened from the ankle, far along your boot towards the ankle. There, it can no longer do its job of

the front-points should project beyond the toe of the boot by ¾ – 1in (1.9 – 2.5cm). A piece of thin card placed at the toe of the boot will show more clearly by how much the front-points project.

Fastening crampon to boot is completed by means of straps or, more recently, cable bindings and 'step-in' bindings. All sorts of patent straps are available. Go for the simplest – four neoprene straps (two per boot) with hole and pin buckles are as good as any (*see Figs 7 and 11*). Whatever your choice, the straps should be of waterproof material or coated in some way to prevent the collection of snow and ice. Crampons are often purchased free of straps, in which case you will have to fit them yourself. This is a simple process. Follow the manufacturer's instructions carefully and remember that all buckles should lie on the outside of the boot so that one set of buckles cannot snag on the other, perhaps tripping an otherwise flawless performance.

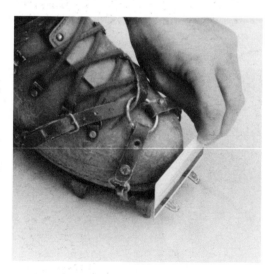

Fig 10   A card shows more clearly how much front-point you have – in this case rather less than half an inch and scarcely enough for anything other than difficult mixed climbing, which is how this particular crampon earns its living.

holding the front of the crampon to the toe of the boot. On the other hand, if that same loop is too small, you may not be able to pull it over the toe of the boot in the first place, in which case it is useless. So arrange your rings with care, and don't take it for granted that, fitting one pair of boots perfectly, they will necessarily fit a second pair. Some makes of boots are bulkier than others, even when they advertise the same foot size.

Crampon straps may be secured to the crampons by tying, threading or riveting; all

Fig 11   Detail of the arrangement of straps and front posts at the toe.

seem to be equally satisfactory. Straps should be tight enough to hold boot and crampon together on the roughest ground, but not so tight that they restrict the foot's circulation. This is a problem with leather boots, less of one with plastic thanks to its rigid shell. Some ankle straps go around the ankle once, others twice. The latter give greater security but whichever you choose, the strap should be long enough after the buckle is fastened to be gripped easily with a gloved hand.

In recent years cable and step-in bindings have improved enormously. When properly fitted – and fitting here is crucial – they are superb, though a sceptical and conservative climbing population may take some time to be won over. Their advantages are:

1.   No straps to break or to restrict circulation, so feet are warmer and safer.
2.   Speed – no fiddling with straps, rings and buckles with frozen fingers.

Their disadvantages are that they must be adjusted to fit perfectly. They tend to fit imperfectly on leather boots because such boots usually lack pronounced welts at heel and toe, which are essential for a secure cable or step-in fitting. On the other hand, most plastic boots have a veritable ledge of a welt at heel and toe, tailor-made for step-in bindings. The two most popular (and the best) step-in bindings of the 1985 – 86 season were to be found on the Salewa Messner crampon and the Grivel F2. Competition should increase the choice and decrease the price. I spent a winter in leather boots trying to kick off a pair of crampons fastened with step-in bindings, without success. Properly fitted they work well, especially on plastic boots.

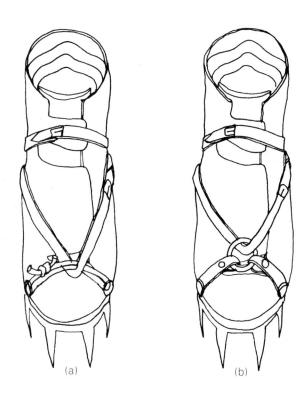

(a)　　　　　(b)

Fig 12　Alternative methods of securing the front posts.

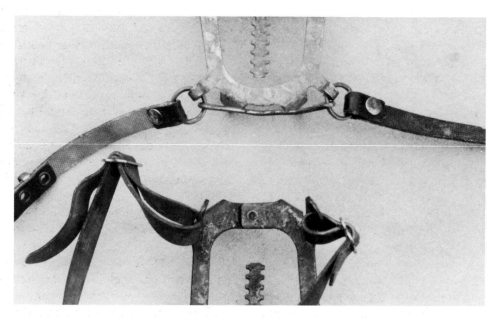

*Fig 13　Two methods of attaching straps to crampons: (top) rivets;
(bottom) Chouinard thread buckles.*

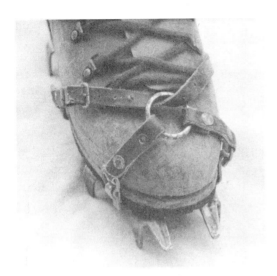

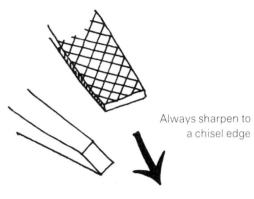

Always sharpen to
a chisel edge

*Fig 14   Details of a toe ring variation
(sometimes called Scots rings).*

Fig 15   Sharpening the front-points.

Care and Maintenance *(Fig 15)*

After use check crampons to see that screws
have not worked loose, that straps or
bindings are in good fettle, and that rivets
etc. are still holding good. Have a look, too,
at the metal of the crampon, checking for
cracks or other signs of metal fatigue –
particularly after heavy use. Check for
sharpness, and re-sharpen only as frequently
as necessary, which may be often if you
alternate climbing on mixed ground with
climbing on ice. Water-ice demands sharp
front-points; snow-ice can be subdued with
blunter instruments. Sharpen by hand with
a file, never with a powered grindstone as
the heat may degrade the temper. Sharpen
the down points to a point and the front-
points from the top to a chisel edge.

Choose your crampons carefully. Fit
them with even greater care and attach them
securely. They turn smooth and potentially
dangerous snow and ice slopes into the
gentlest and friendliest of places.

ICE-AXES

The axe is the most important tool in the ice
climber's trade and there is a bewildering
array to choose from. Fortunately most of
the modern axes on the retailer's shelf work
well enough under most circumstances.
Proof of that, if proof is needed, is supplied
by any cluster of mountaineers. Ask any ten
which axe they prefer and you'll probably
get ten different answers. Take some comfort from the discord – it means that almost
any modern axe will do for almost everything, but some useful information will help
you make a choice.

It used to be simpler, and not so many
years ago – twenty, at most. At that time all
axes had wooden shafts, usually very long
ones, and they all had picks emerging, more
or less, at right angles from the shaft. On
gentle slopes they were little more than
walking sticks; on steeper slopes they cut
holds for hand and foot. These uses dictated
the length and shape of the axe. Then – and

it is difficult to say precisely when or where – a revolution occurred. Of this revolution Chouinard says in *Climbing Ice*:

'On a rainy summer day in 1966, I went on to a glacier in the Alps with the purpose of testing every different type of ice-axe available at the time. My plan was to see which one worked best for *piolet ancre*, which one was better at step-cutting, and why. After I found a few answers, it took the intervention of Donald Snell to convince the very reluctant and conservative Charlet factory to make a 55cm axe with a curved pick for the crazy American. In those days a 55cm axe was crazy enough – but a curved pick! I had the feeling that modifying the standard straight pick into a curve compatible with the arc of the axe's swing would allow the pick to stay put better in the ice. I had noticed that a standard pick would often pop out when I placed my weight on it. My idea worked'.

A few years later Rob Collister wrote in *Mountain*:

'The development of a curved pick for axes and hammers was an event in ice climbing history comparable with the introduction of crampons in the 1890s, or the use of front-points and ice pitons in the 1930s. It could prove more revolutionary than either. Since it makes for both greater speed and security, it will encourage those who have previously been deterred by the need to choose between the two'.

Doubtless the French, Germans and Austrians have their version of this revolution too, but sometime in the later 1960s axes changed shape. Axe picks were drooped. Chouinard achieved this by *curving*

the picks steeply downward; MacInnes (on his prototype Terrordactyls) by *angling* his picks steeply downwards, at an angle of about 55 degrees between pick and shaft. Using these new tools a climber could hang his entire weight on an axe and it wouldn't pop out – even on vertical ice. This meant that instead of climbing ice by hours of laborious step-cutting, a climber with a new axe in either hand could attack the steepest ice front on, the most natural way.

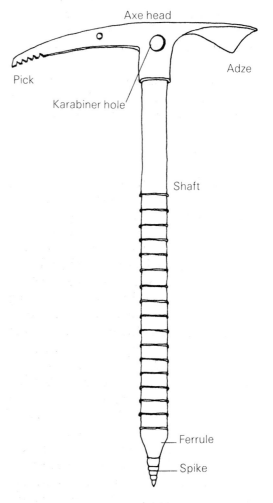

Fig 16   A typical ice-axe.

Chouinard claims, and he may well be right, that this technique was first used in California in 1967. The French christened it '*piolet traction*'. The English-speaking world call it front-pointing. The effect was dramatic. Times for routes were halved, then decimated. Two, three and four routes a day became commonplace where, 'pre-revolution', one a day had been the accepted ration. Even the hardest winter routes were soloed – such was the efficiency and security afforded by these new tools – and step-cutting died a short death, despite attempts by traditionalists to drag it out for an indecently long time. I have never cut an ice step in my life except in demonstration, though the odd one can still be used to good effect. The ice-axe and its relatives such as the ice-hammer merit closer inspection.

The Shaft

1. *Material*: the traditional shaft was of ash or hickory. Its day has passed. Laminated bamboo enjoyed a short vogue, particularly on Chouinard axes. Few modern axes are wooden-shafted, although there are able climbers who still prefer the feel of a good, straight-grained hickory shaft. Fibreglass has been used for making shafts, though they have never proved to be really popular. Perhaps the feel is not right or folk are wary of the variation in strength to which this material is prone at low temperatures. A coating of fibreglass can also be used to strengthen any wooden-shafted axe, but at the cost of greater weight. The most common materials for today's axe shafts are metal – aluminium and titanium being recent contenders – and carbonfibre, which is more recent still. A bare metal shaft is cold to hold, and cold hands must be avoided. Coating a metal shaft in a moulded rubber or neoprene grip largely solves this problem, as well as giving the axe a better feel and dampening most of the vibration consequent upon a hefty blow to hard ice.

2. *Length*: the ideal length for an ice-axe shaft is one of those subjects of perennial – and often heated – debate amongst climbers. No two people seem to agree, and when they do, one will quickly change his mind. As a rough guide only, 2ft 4in (70cm) is generally held to be the order of length for an alpine axe – the spike just scrapes the ground when it is held in the hand at the axe head. Then, again roughly, the steeper the climb, or the more confined its nature, the shorter the axe. The shortest anyone would want to go is 1ft 2½in (36cm) (the length of a Terrordactyl shaft), and many prefer something comparatively long, perhaps 1ft 10in – 2ft 2in (55–65cm) even on vertical ice. It is a matter of individual preference and some experience – not much more. If it helps, I have climbed on everything from Scottish gullies, to Welsh water-ice, to Alpine north faces, to K2 with the same two axes for the last ten years. They both have 1ft 4in (40cm) shafts and although I have flirted with others, I always return to them. Some use two short axes for steep technical ground, but a longer (2ft 4in, or 70cm) axe for alpine work. The permutations are endless – as are the arguments. Start on steep ice with two 1ft 4in – 1ft 8in (40–50cm) tools and you won't go far wrong. A shaft with a flattened oval cross-section is the most comfortable shape to hold, while a ribbed, rubber moulding gives a better grip.

The Head (Pick and Adze)

Most of today's heads are made from high-quality steel. It matters little whether they are of chrome molybidenum, chrome vanadium or titanium, they all work well. Balance and weight are important, however. It is not uncommon to see a climbing shop filled with climbers carefully fondling axes as a gun-fighter might his guns, or scything the air in an imaginary move on some imaginary climb as a gladiator might practise a swipe with his chosen weapon. Once again, only experience will enable you to make an educated selection. Ask friends, solicit opinions of those more experienced, borrow before you buy.

A problem with opinions is that they vary. While some prefer heavy-headed axes, arguing that they make for a penetrating blow, others choose light heads, arguing that every ounce saved is energy conserved. There's no absolute answer. My axe has weights that I can attach to the head by means of an allen screw, so I am able to make it lighter or heavier as the whim takes me. In fact, I've climbed with all four weights on, and all four off, and have found the difference negligible.

Pick Profiles

There are three basic pick profiles – curved, inclined or angled, and banana, which is really an inclined pick with a bit of French flair added – to some good effect. There is not much to choose between them. I prefer inclined or banana picks but wouldn't lose any sleep if invited to climb with a curve. I have never conducted a survey, but I suspect that curves are more popular than angles on moderate and Alpine ground, while angles (or banana) are the preferred shape on steeper

stuff. I am told that there is now an 'elephant' pick. This is S-shaped. Its relationship to jumbo is not obvious unless it is in the trunk. I am told that such picks work well, although not discernibly better than bananas. The ingenuity of man and the fecundity of his terminology suggest that there is plenty of scope for more exotic breeding. At the moment it looks as if ornithologists rule the nominal roost – vultures, eagles, Terrordactyls – with zoologists, vegetarians and fishmongers filling the minor placings with chacals, bananas and barracudas.

Most axes for serious climbing are equipped with picks, whatever their profile, at about 55–65 degrees to the shaft, and they all work. Picks should be thin (for penetration) but strong – no easy combination. A set of teeth – no more than four or five are really needed – should feature on the underside at the tip. These teeth stop the axe from wobbling in the ice; they are not there to prevent the pick from slipping out, as the angle of the pick alone does that. Many manufacturers, Simond on his Chacal and Barracuda tools included, cut their teeth too long. After some experimentation you may find that you want to file down some of the more aggressive fangs. I reduced those on my own axe to less than half the original length before I could extract it with anything less than a monumental effort. A good axe should go in easily, stay in, and come out when asked. An axe which takes more effort to extract than insert needs to be doctored, or de-tuned. But go slowly; it is more difficult to re-cut the teeth than it is to remove them. A favourite axe of mine had but three tiny milk teeth. The angle of its pick was steep and it held in ice without worry, allowing itself to be withdrawn without persuasion. Since then, the manufacturers,

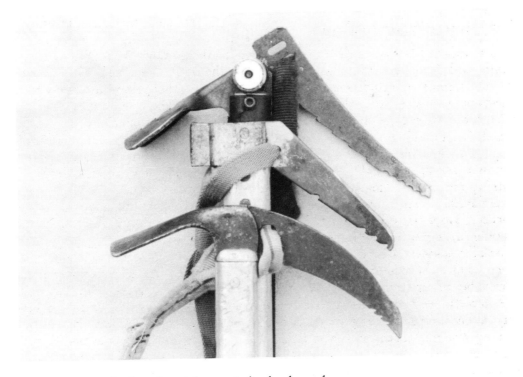

Fig 17   Three picks (from the top): banana, inclined and curved.

bowing to fashion rather than efficacy, have serrated the thing along its entire under length. It looks like Jaws and works no better than the original.

The banana pick (*see Fig 17*) is really a modification of the inclined pick and is designed to make extraction easier, although not everyone agrees that it achieves this. In my opinion banana picks work well, although since that opinion is based on experience all too often gained *in extremis*, it is difficult to be sure whether its efficiency is the result of a good design or a good day. Certainly a trembling 100ft run out is no laboratory test.

Adzes

Adzes are designed primarily for one of two jobs. Large, shovel-like, steeply inclined adzes, such as those found on the Terrordactyl and Barracuda axes, are made for climbing steep, less than solid snow, where the rule is the more steeply inclined the adze (up to 60 degrees), and the bigger, the better. Such adzes will cut ice and snow for steps but not as well as a more conventional adze which was made for that job. Conventional adzes are correspondingly less efficient when climbing less than solid snow. My choice would be a Terrordactyl/Barracuda-type adze which will do very well for the few steps you are likely to cut. Secondary tasks, which both types of adze perform satis-

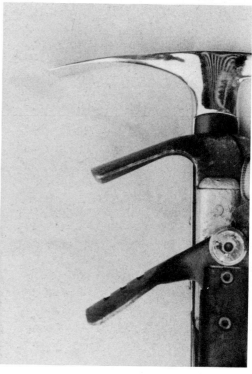

(a)   *(b)*

Fig 18   Three adzes of differing size, shape and angle: (top) an old-fashioned step-cutting adze; (middle) a general purpose adze on a Clog 'vulture'; (bottom) a front-pointing adze on a Simond 'Barracuda'.

factorily, include chopping stances at belays and clearing away soft or rotten snow and ice in order to reveal the good stuff in which to place ice-screws.

Specialised Picks and Adzes

Jeff Lowe, the celebrated and innovative American ice climber has developed an axe with a pick which is a hollow tube. He christened it the Hummingbird. It was designed with steep water-ice in mind and that is where it works best – the hollow tube displacing less ice than a conventional pick which makes it both easier to place and less likely to shatter cold, brittle ice. Unless you intend to climb exclusively on frozen waterfalls, however, such a weapon is almost certainly more specialised than you need.

Another good ice climbing axe boasts a long solid spike (about the thickness of a pencil) for a pick. Again this works well in ice or very solid snow, but is not as versatile as a conventional pick. More and more manufacturers are furnishing axes (and hammers) with interchangeable picks. Clearly these are the most versatile of the lot,

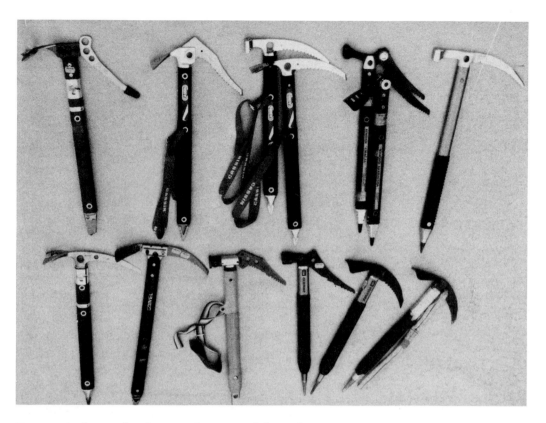

Fig 19 A selection of modern ice tools: (top row, left to right) Camp Hyper Couloir; Cassin Ice Fall; Cassin Extreme (axe and hammer); Simond Barracuda (axe) and Chacal (hammer); Snowdon Mouldings Curver; (bottom row, left to right) Camp Gabarrou; Grivel Super Courmayeur; Stubai Steep Ice; Clog Vampire (hammer) and Vulture (axe); Clog Vulture (early model).

but be sure to fasten your selected pick well. A loose pick is disconcerting; a lost one disastrous.

Spikes

Spikes are pretty much spikes. They should be kept reasonably sharp for penetrating snow up to névé consistency, but not weapon-sharp, when they can be dangerous, to mates as well as to the owner. A karabiner hole in the spike (or in the lower end of the shaft) is useful for clipping into in order to rest on very steep ice – a technique we will

look at later.

Ice Hammers

Modern ice hammers are essentially axes with a hammer-head in the place of the adze. Most climbers carry one of each: an adze in case steps have to be cut or in case loose snow is encountered; a hammer for driving pitons, snargs, etc. Axes and hammers may or may not be the same length; again it's a matter of preference. Some climbers carry three tools (useful on long climbs if one tool breaks), in which case the combination is likely to be two axes and one hammer. Two adzes are twice as good as one in unconsolidated or melting snow, and it is possible, if not entirely satisfactory, to drive pitons and snargs and to start ice-screws with an axe if your hammer breaks. Only a pessimist, and a rich one at that, would carry two of each.

Maintenance

Keep your ice tools rust-free and sharpen them as often as necessary with a hard file. Stick to the original shape, although, as previously mentioned, some long-toothed picks will benefit from a certain amount of de-tuning. Avoid the use of power tools for they will degrade the temper of the metal. Tradition has it that old-timers carry a file on their person so that some sharpening of crampons and axe can be conducted *en route*. I have yet to spot this in practice, but it is not a bad habit.

Tools that have adjustable or interchangeable components should be checked daily to see that screws and bolts are all snug.

SLINGS/WRIST LOOPS

For climbing on steep ground, your axes and hammers will need to be equipped with a sling and wrist loop. You may buy your tool with the maker's sling already in place. These are generally more than adequate. They are easy to replace with a new one when worn or, if you prefer, a home-made version. Half or one-inch (1.25 or 2.5cm) climbing tape is ideal for this purpose and if you are adept at DIY, you can engineer a loop with a local broadening around the wrist in order to reduce pressure and increase comfort. Hands will be warmer too because their blood supply will be less restricted – a

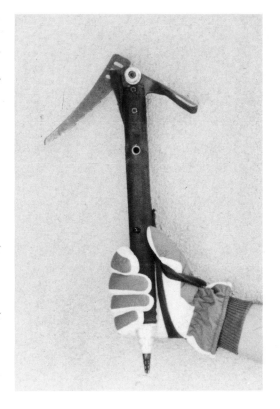

Fig 20   One method of holding the wrist loop.

blood supply that has a hard time flowing uphill all day as it is.

Whether patent or home-made, the sling should be of such a length that when you hold it in your preferred manner, your fist encircles the shaft very close to its end. Try climbing when holding the shaft about half-way up and you'll quickly appreciate how much more efficient it is to hold it at the end. Some like to rest by crooking their elbow into the wrist loop, in which case the loop has to be big enough to take the owner's forearm, encased, as it is likely to be, in several layers of sleeve.

out of it. The argument is a reasonable one. My only objection to a mid-shaft attachment is a difficulty that arises on mixed ground when axes that have been dropped to your wrists, there to dangle, while your hands seize holds, are likely to dangle horizontally

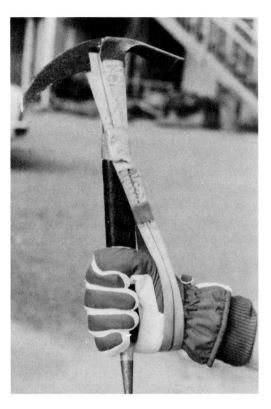

Fig 21   An alternative method of holding the wrist loop.

Point of Attachment

A wrist loop is usually attached to the axe at one of two points; at the head or at some point along the shaft (though always above the hand). All axes will have a hole or slot through which the wrist loop may be knotted (always using a tape knot), and here lies the root of another argument: *where to attach*.

Those who prefer to attach to a hole provided at some point in the shaft claim that this ensures that the wrist loop, when weighted, will follow the line of the shaft more faithfully, and that this, in turn, encourages the pick into the ice, rather than

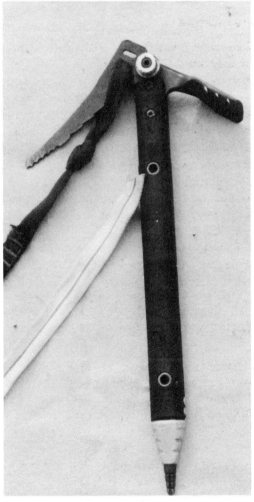

Fig 22   Two points of attachment on a Barracuda axe. A wrist loop has been attached to a slot in the head. The white tape leads to a hole by which the manufacturers intended the attachment to be made.

and catch in the mountainside. I have such an axe, a Barracuda, and have chosen to ignore the maker's preferred attachment hole about two-thirds of the way up the shaft because on mixed ground it caught with infuriating efficiency. I have attached the wrist loop to the head, where there is a slot, though whether it is provided for that purpose I do not know. No matter, the axe is now a model of convenience, dangles harmlessly vertical from the wrist, and the three inches (7.5cm) between the two possible points of attachment make no difference that I can discern.

If, by attaching your wrist loop to the head of your axe (or hammer), you are worried that the resultant pull may not be in the same axis as the shaft – that is, straight downwards – then you can tape the wrist loop (with sticky tape), or tie it (with line or climbing tape in a small loop), to the shaft, a few inches above the hand.

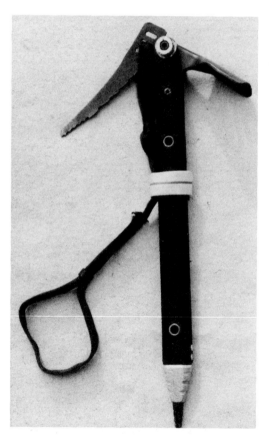

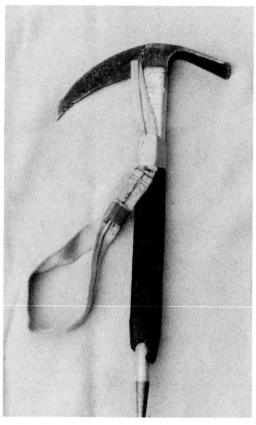

Fig 23   *A loop sewn around the shaft and stitched into the wrist loop (to stop it riding up or down independently of the wrist loop). Although snug, such a loop should be free to travel up the shaft if the climber wishes to move to a daggering position.*

Fig 24   *Much the same result can be achieved with sticky tape. The tape should not be positioned so low on the shaft that the climber cannot grasp the head without relinquishing the wrist loop.*

Other methods of achieving this involve winding the wrist loop around the shaft. I do not recommend these because, whilst the winding is an easy enough operation standing on the ground at the beginning of a climb, it is a considerable evolution *in extremis*, after you have let go of your axes in order to use your hands, for whatever reason. Using more conventional 'straight' wrist loops, axes that have been dropped to the wrist can be brought to hand simply with a flick of that wrist.

My last point on this subject is that more people these days climb with axes that are so short that the inches difference between a shaft attachment and a head attachment are fairly unimportant. *See* Front-pointing (pages 50 to 57) and Mixed Ground (pages 62 to 65) to complete the wrist loop story. Doubtless this facet of the attachment controversy will rage all the more fiercely for the views that I have expressed.

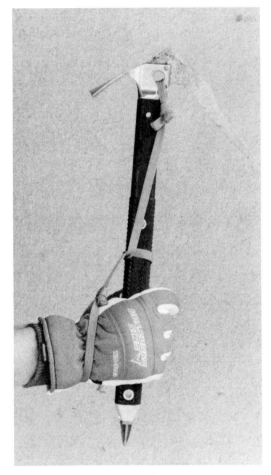 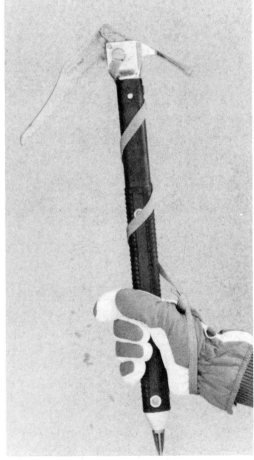

(a)   *(b)*

Fig 25   Two more ways of keeping the wrist loop along the axis of the shaft.

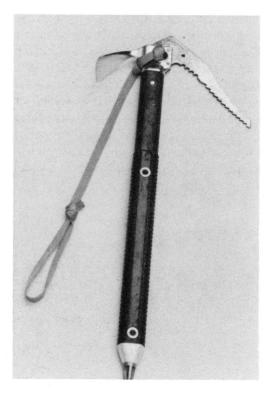 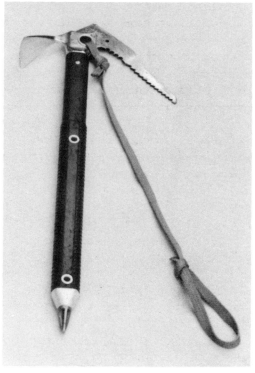

Fig 26   Not the best way in which to attach a wrist loop to the head of an axe. A downwards pull on the wrist loop will tend to pull the pick back out of its hole in the ice.

Fig 27   Better to attach the loop from the front of the shaft. Weight applied to this wrist loop will pull the pick into the ice.

Sling Use

Axe slings should be carefully checked for wear and tear. There will be times when your entire weight (and therefore life) hangs on them and a shredded sling is an unnecessary excitement. Opinions vary on the desirability of using an axe sling on less steep or walking terrain. The disadvantages are:

1.   The axe follows you closely if you fall and may clout body and head during the descent, although you shouldn't be falling on this sort of ground.

2.   It is awkward to change from hand to hand when zigzagging up snow slopes (when the axe is best carried on the inside hand).

The advantages are:

1.   It is conveniently to hand.
2.   It is difficult to lose.
3.   It affords some support when step-cutting.

On steep ground the sling and wrist loop are such an essential part of the axe and of the climbing technique employed that dissent is plain daft.

Another argument rages over whether axes held in hand by sling and wrist loop should be further secured to the body by a long sling or line, long enough not to restrict an arms-length reach. Here the dis-advantages are:

1. The axe follows closely if you fall and may punish you severely for your error or bad luck.
2. The sling tangles easily (some would say incessantly, and still others would add, in-extricably) with body and equipment.

The advantages are:

1. Once your fall has been arrested you know where to find your axe (you may even be impaled on it).
2. It can be cast aside with impunity to deal with a rock handhold, or to attend to equipment or bodily functions, and it can be readily retrieved.
3. If the long sling or line is strong enough and of the right length it can be used to hang in for a rest. I have seen ice climbers who have contrived a sling which joins them to their axe. It can be adjusted by means of a single pull through a simple buckle so that it can be snugged-up in order to hang by it for a breather. Since I have never been able to contemplate so complicated a manoeuvre it would be equally unfair were I to commend or condemn. It seems sensible to master the simple things first, then by all means give it a go if you wish.
4. The axe can still be swapped from hand to hand.

If axe or hammer need to be stowed for some period this is best done by means of a holster attached to the harness, although old-timers insist that it is as well to push the axe down between sac and back from over one shoulder. Whether holster or shoulder borne, care should be taken not to drop the implement. If you anticipate that you are stowing your axe for some time, slide it into the compression straps found on the side of most modern rucksacks, rather than attach-ing it to the ice-axe loops at the rear, where, once attached, the ice-axe will be uselessly inaccessible.

CLOTHING

'The uniform 'e wore were nothing
much before
And rather less than 'alf o' that be'ind.'
'Cells', Rudyard Kipling

Snow and ice climbing is, rather obviously, a cool business. Sometimes it's downright cold, and occasionally, just to confound the best of us, it's downright hot. It seems to me that the perverse but ineluctable rule is that you will always either be too hot, or too cold, and usually too hot when moving, too cold when still. The best compromise is to wrap up well at the foot of the climb (particularly in Scotland in winter) and hope that the body's thermostat does its job tolerably well.

Suggesting what might be worn is a risky business for, as if climbers' prejudices and idiosyncrasies weren't enough to deal with, we now have the dictates of fashion thrown into the sartorial shemozzle. I advise, from the feet upwards:

1. Gaiters. Super-gaiters are warmer and dryer.
2. At least one pair of socks (or stockings, if breeches are worn). Many prefer two. It is

a mistake, however, to cram your feet with too much cover. Tight feet are constricted feet, constricted feet are cold feet, and cold feet can be frost-bitten feet.

3. Long johns of polypropylene or thin pile or wool.

4. Breeches, or wind or waterproof over-trousers, or ski salopettes. The latter are warm, light and windproof and make ideal winter climbing wear, even if they are a little flimsy.

5. Vests, shirts and pullovers to taste.

6. Wind or waterproof jacket or anorak.

7. Thin polyester or silk gloves as inners under thicker, warmer mitts. The mitts are best equipped with elastic wrist loops so they can dangle safely from wrists while the wearer fumbles with a knot, karabiner, or crampon strap with inner-gloved fingers.

8. Balaclava or other woolly hat (under a helmet – stand under any leader for more than a few seconds and you'll be convinced of the value of a hard hat).

9. Scarf (silk if you are so inclined).

10. Something spare in your rucksack for your torso (*see* page 103 for more suggestions on rucksack contents).

The choice of clothing, most of it functional, to be found in today's outdoor stores is, almost literally, bedazzling. No longer do winter climbers go to the hills in a uniformly drab grey and khaki. Rather, they go as brightly strutting peacocks, colourful, if coy, and climbing standards go inexorably upwards too. Is there a connection? I doubt it, but it's fun.

OTHER PARAPHERNALIA

As I have already explained, I am assuming that you have some knowledge of rock climbing, so ropes, harness, slings, nuts, etc. will not be enlarged upon. Kit unique to winter climbing, such as ice-screws, snargs and deadmen are dealt with in other chapters (for those three subjects, *see* Chapter 3).

2 Snow and Ice Skills

For the purpose of becoming familiar with the balance and feel of an ice-axe . . . the axe may be thrown into the air, caused to revolve a determined number of times, and caught on the descent, in either hand, as a good step-cutter should be ambidextrous.'

Harold Raeburn

'Then I lost my grip of the axe and it started somersaulting in the air with both my arms windmilling trying to grab it and my feet scarting about in crumbly holds . . . we shambled down number four gully and I found my axe.'

Robin Smith

CLIMBING WITH CRAMPONS

Introduction

Volumes have been written about the business of climbing with crampons – some of it good, some of it unnecessary, some of it turning a fairly straightforward skill into a black art, and some of it mumbo-jumbo. It is my considered advice that the best way to learn how to use crampons is to put them on and to go out and play with them: on the flat, on easy slopes, on short, steeper slopes and on very short, very steep slopes; up, down, sideways left and sideways right, diagonally left and right and every which way. Play until you are as at home with your crampons on ice as you would be in carpet slippers on a rug. Play until you have exhausted the process of discovery of what

the front-points will do, what the down points will do, how steep you can go without hands and how steep with hands. Have some fun. It will take a few minutes, perhaps a few hours, before they no longer feel strange. Keep at it until you can dance a jig on a 40-degree slope, and then you'll be ready to climb in your crampons. You may trip or fall – it doesn't matter in a safe place. I know a very good ice climber, an instructor of ice climbing indeed, who fell on a patch of spirit-level horizontal ice on the footpath leading to Ben Nevis. His nose bled badly. We laughed a lot. He climbs Grade 5 with ease.

The following points are distilled from all that might be said about climbing with crampons.

You may hear of a French technique (which isn't half as exciting as it sounds), a German technique and an American crampon technique – almost everyone, it seems, claims to have invented a technique. Ignore all the names – it is only the method that matters. The problem is that the French think they invented the art of using crampons (which they probably did) and have been bent on inflicting their code on the rest of the climbing world ever since. The Germans think they re-invented it all (which they probably did) and have been bent on doing everything better and faster than the French (which they don't). As Chouinard comments in *Climbing on Snow and Ice*:

'The sixties were the age of super-nationalism in Alpine sports. This was especially true in skiing, where there were Austrian,

Fig 28   Ample, easy angled ice.

Fig 29   Sparse, steep ice.

French, and even American techniques. The French, with their 10-point crampons, were artfully angling and flat-footing their way up the big snow faces of the Mont Blanc range, while the Austrians and Germans were tiptoeing around on only their front-points. In 1969 the leading spokesman for ice climbing in France, André Contamine, wrote in the journal *La Montagne*: "The *piolet ancre* is one of the most useful techniques of the alpinist. It permits him to cover ground on the steepest slopes without fatigue or difficulty. It is the key to cramponing French style". Two years later the Austrian climber, Wastl Mariner, wrote in the same journal: "The most natural technique anatomically, and the most secure and sparing of energy, is to advance on steep ice on the front-points of 12-point crampons – called front-pointing". He went on to criticise the French technique for being un-natural and difficult to learn. This caused an absolute furore at the *Ecole National de Ski et Alpinisme* in Chamonix, when rebellious students posted the article on the bulletin board!'

It seems more sensible not to worry about such arcana as *pied assis* or *en canard* (unless you know what a duck is) and to do what comes easiest and most naturally – fore-armed with a little reading and rearmed with a little experience.

Donning Crampons

Stories of competent climbers getting half-way up a route before attempting to put on crampons on some ridiculously steep slope or exiguous ledge are legion. Put crampons on whilst still on easy ground – you will seldom regret it, and if you do you can always take them off again. If they have modern step-in bindings, putting them on is easy. Lay them on the ground, or snow if it presents a firm surface, or a rock or a rucksack if it doesn't, and push the toe wire forward and the heel clip back. Step in. Locate the toe wire in the welt of the boot. Place the heel piece on the welt at the heel and lever into position. Correctly fitted, it should click into position with a suggestion of a snap. Step-in bindings don't have to be very tight and it should take no perceptible effort to snap the heel piece home. This done, fasten the safety strap around the ankle, repeat the operation on the other foot, give them both a good shake, check them visually – and away you go.

Life is not much more complicated with more conventional straps. Lay crampons on a firm surface, position all rings and straps outboard of posts, step in, fasten front straps, fasten ankle straps, and check. Away you go. (*See* Chapter 1 for the various methods of fastening straps.)

Crampon Techniques

1. *Easy ground*. Walk more or less as normal. You'll soon become accustomed to being an inch or so taller and to your boot soles being effectively an inch or so deeper. Remember that you have ten downward facing points – the more points you are able to use, the greater security you gain. Instead of edging feet, as you would naturally in boots without crampons, allow your ankles to roll out from the slope so that the soles of your boots lie at the same angle as the slope and all ten points are encouraged to bite.

2. *Moderate ground: slopes up to 55 degrees.* Going up doing what comes naturally in these circumstances means using the feet flat on the ground. Because of the ground's angle, this entails placing the feet across the

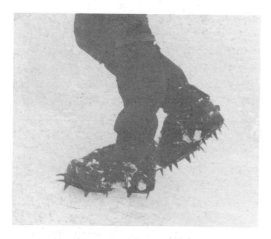

Fig 30   Crampons on an easy angled ice slope; ten points working.

slope, walking sideways, and zigzagging to stay on course, sharing the work-load between both legs. Changing direction from a zag to a zig and vice versa needs practice, but soon it will be second nature. You will also become accustomed to bringing the lower foot past the upper (and in front of it) in a sort of crabwise step. On the steepest ground, on which such a gait is practical, this may mean that you are almost 'advancing backwards' and it is then time to turn inwards and front-point.

Sometimes, particularly on angles approaching 55 degrees, the most natural thing to do is to side-step with the lower foot while front-pointing with the upper

Fig 31   Crampons at work descending an easy slope.

Fig 32   Aid Burgess is able to keep all ten points in contact with the ice by slightly bending the knees and sitting back.

Fig 33   The steeper the slope, the greater the knee bend...

Fig 34   ... and the deeper the squat.

Fig 35   Descending an easy angled slope: sit back slightly to keep all down points in contact with the snow or ice; the axe is at the ready.

Fig 36   Cramponing up an easy angled slope with feet flat and using the axe as a third leg.

foot. Try it – it's not nearly as difficult as it sounds. Clearly the ice-axe plays a big part on ground of intermediate steepness and beyond. Its function will be explained shortly. In practice, crampons and axe are seldom divorced.

3. *Traversing*. Simply walk or climb sideways, feet still flat and encouraging all down points to bite by rolling the ankle of the outboard foot pronouncedly outwards. If you lack flexibility in the ankles, you may find traversing easier if you point the toe of the lower foot downhill, with the foot still flat

on the slope. As the slope steepens, both feet will tend to point downhill. If this feels natural, use them both that way.

4. *Climbing down*. It is quicker (and after practice, easier) to continue to face outwards for as long as nerve and angle allow – and both should allow up to 50 degrees at least. On your first day at play on safe snow slopes and ice boulders it is worth practising descents facing outwards. You will probably surprise yourself at the steepness of slopes that can be safely and quickly negotiated in this way. But it does take

Fig 37 *Standing in balance on a moderate slope (actually quite a steep moderate slope).*

Fig 38 *Moving up or across. Note how the ankle of the lower (and outer) foot is rolled outwards in order to keep ten down points working. The body is centred (more or less) directly over the feet and crampons.*

practice, especially on hard ice.

You will soon discover that in order to have all ten down points working you have to sit back; and that the steeper the slope, the more pronounced this squat will be. Play with the axe too and discover all the ways that it can help you, from being placed spike down, hand on axe head, walking stick-like below or to the side; to being held, hand in sling, and hooked (by the pick) behind on steeper steps. When you are no longer comfortable descending facing out it is time to turn in to the slope.

5. *Steep ground*. The easiest and most natural way in which to use crampons on steep ground is to face it square-on and climb on front-points – up, sideways or down. Once again, play games in safe places to discover just how steep a slope you can climb, traverse and descend on front-points alone – only hands for balance: no axe.

The Germans call climbing on front-points the 'German technique'. Everyone else calls it front-pointing except the French who have christened it *'pied en avant'*. This technique is speedy, simple and perhaps the

(a)   *(b)*

Fig 39 Descending moderate ground, knees well bent, squat fairly pronounced (and ungainly!).

(a)   *(b)*

Fig 40   Descending moderate ground: (a) the axe is for balance and not much more; (b) in this case all twelve points are contributing to purchase.

most obvious of all crampon techniques – a fortunate circumstance since it is the one you will be using most when climbing. Take care to place or tap your foot on the ice, as a kick may shatter the ice and will give you no better purchase than a deft tap. (Unless you are prepared to work on a budget of two big toenails per winter it pays to keep toenails short – or your boots long – as all that kicking in the ice brings the two together and percussion and toenails don't mix.) Keep boot and crampons square to the slope so that both front-points are sharing the work. Once you are satisfied that the foot is there to stay, transfer all your weight on to,

and over, it. To begin with, this may take several taps and some soul searching, but later one tap and a stiff dose of conviction will usually suffice. Then repeat the procedure with the other foot. It is important that you stand on and over the working crampon, as it is your own body weight that presses the front-points to the ice. The more weight you place on them, the more they will bite. Boldness has great virtue in it. Keep the feet flat – actually at right angles to the slope. A raised heel levers the front-points out of the ice, while too low a heel has the same effect when the climber stretches to move up (*see Fig 49*). Once positioned, keep

Fig 41 Having fun and making friends with crampons and ice. This is fair enough, but in time ground at this angle (about 45 degrees) is more efficiently negotiated by side-stepping with at least the lower foot flat.

the foot still – movement only weakens the ice in which the crampon is lodged. In practice you will find that, except on near vertical water-ice, you are seldom standing on the front-points alone. More often the load is shared by the two front-points and the first set of down points (immediately behind the front-points on most crampons).

With only a little experience you will find that you rarely confine yourself to one crampon technique for more than a few moves. On moderate ground, short sections of front-pointing gain height quickly and rest the muscles you have been exercising in zigzagging, though at some cost to the calves. On even the steepest climbs it is often possible to give one foot or the other a rest from pure front-pointing and every opportunity should be taken to rest the calves by standing on natural holds – ledges, bulges, holes – or by scraping a side foothold with the crampon. This can be done even on vertical ice (*see Fig 50*). It is probably only on waterfalls, vertically frozen, that pure front-pointing is used for entire pitches, and even then it will be a rare pitch where it is employed exclusively. By now you will have found that crampons work in dozens of ways at dozens of angles. Use the

Fig 42   Steep ice: standing in balance and discovering what can be done 'pied en avant'.

Fig 43   Steeper ice...

Fig 44   ...moving up...

Fig 45   ...and standing on the working crampon.

Fig 46   Presenting front-points to steep ice...

Fig 47   ... well-positioned feet and crampons.

Fig 48   Steep ice: badly positioned feet caused by stepping uncomfortably high. This overstepping has resulted in both heels being lifted.

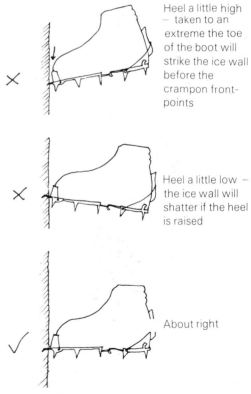

Heel a little high — taken to an extreme the toe of the boot will strike the ice wall before the crampon front-points

Heel a little low — the ice wall will shatter if the heel is raised

About right

Fig 49   Positioning the front-points in the ice.

Fig 50   A side hold scraped with a crampon and a rest won for the left calf.

entire repertoire, resting legs and feet at every opportunity. Remember: a change is often as good as a rest.

CLIMBING WITH AXE AND CRAMPONS

In the not-so-old days, and bad not-so-old days they must have been, progress on steep ice was made by cramponing in the ways that have been described and, at the same time, using the axe to cut holds on which to pull and push with the hands. Upward progress was understandably slow, purchase tenuous, the effort exhausting and the skills elusive. The need to cut handholds was reduced in the 1950s by the use of ice daggers with which the climber literally stabbed the ice, so that the dagger, once stabbed, became a handhold. Then some thought of drooping, and others of curving the picks of axes and hammers. The effect was the same – dramatic. These new profile axes could be hooked into the snow or ice as a perfect and mobile hold in either hand. The ice climbing revolution had come, the ice climbing world was never to be the same again, and the art and practice of cutting steps and handholds died a very natural death – though some still maintain that reports of its death are exaggerated.

There is a school of thought that catalogues all the positions for carrying an axe and all the ways in which it may be used to assist progress. The many obscure names that accompany these techniques – *Piolet Panne*, *Piolet Ramasse*, etc. – seem to complicate the whole business unnecessarily and unhelpfully.

Walking and Gentle Slopes

On very easy ground carry the axe as you please. Indeed, it may be that it remains attached to your rucksack. On moderate slopes the axe can be used as a kind of third leg: hold it by the head, always in the uphill hand where it will be nearer to the snow, and use it for support.

44

*Fig 51 Walking with crampons and axe (in bucket steps) near the top
of the North Face of the Eiger. Climber: Dave Nicholls.*

There are those who spend happy hours arguing whether, when the axe is used in this way, the pick should face forwards or backwards. It matters not. One may prove more comfortable than the other, or you may decide that one is the more natural position from which to perform self-arrest. Try both and take your choice. If you can find no reason to discriminate then it is suggested that you make a habit of carrying the axe with the pick pointing backwards. That way, should you slip, the pick will be in a ready position. Try it; I think the argument will soon be clear.

It is not always necessary (or desirable) to don crampons at the first sniff of a snow slope, though crampons nearly always afford an advantage on ice of any angle.

Without crampons steps can be kicked in snow just as you would kick a football, for hours on end, with the axe for support in your uphill hand and ready to be deployed in self-arrest if need be.

When kicking steps, a lazy rhythm will make life easier. Those following should use the same steps and enjoy the ride. As long as a reasonable kick produces a step deep enough to accommodate a third of the boot it makes perfectly good sense to proceed in this way. If, because of the hardness of the snow, you are only able to lodge an inch or so, life will probably be easier wearing crampons. Safety and economy of effort are the two considerations – weigh them and decide. Sometimes it's a toss-up – no matter.

Intermediate Slopes

On steeper slopes (say 35 – 50 degrees) the axe can be used as a brace. Hold it across your body with the uphill hand near the spike end of the shaft and pressing down and into the slope. The other hand holds the head. Used with crampons, feet flat, surprisingly steep moves can be made.

On ground steeper still (up to 60 degrees), the axe can be used in an anchor position, as shown in *Figs 56* and *57*.

Of these, the last two techniques are the least natural in the ice climbing game so some practice will probably be necessary before you feel at ease with them. In any case they are not much more than useful adjuncts to the full-blown front-pointing technique, the method by which you are likely to conduct 90 per cent of your snow and ice climbing beyond the walk to or from the climb.

Fig 52   Kicking steps – no crampons yet.

Fig 53   Bracing on an intermediate slope.

Fig 54   Bracing to rest on an intermediate slope.

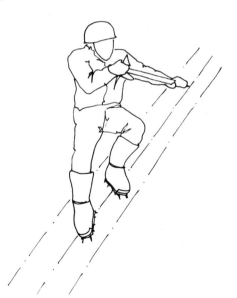

Fig 55   Bracing will work on fairly steep slopes (up to 50 degrees). The inside leg is being brought through. Note that the lower foot is pointing down the slope so that ten points bite.

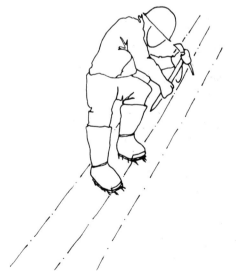

Fig 56   When anchoring on steeper slopes, you will find yourself almost going backwards. It is nearly time to turn square-on and front-point.

(a)

(b)

(c)

(d)

Fig 57   Climbing and traversing by anchoring the ice-axe.

Fig 58   *Proof! Balti porters bracing with their staves in the Braldu Gorge, Karakoram.*

Steep Slopes

Front-pointing is probably what most of us have in mind when we think of ice climbing. It is wonderfully straightforward, with probably not much more to it than would occur to most folk naturally if they were invited to put on crampons, take up two axes and climb a 65 – 75 degree snow or ice slope. There are, however, a number of matters worthy of consideration. The first is, as you will have found when playing on ice in crampons, that you can get up surprisingly steep slopes without an axe at all. The next thing to do is to find out how steeply you can climb with one axe and only then move on to play the game with two – or an axe and a hammer. I make this point because I have often seen climbers front-pointing by laboriously planting both axes before moving up, on ground that really only deserved one and, in some cases, no axe at all. And this only matters because it wastes both time and energy.

Fig 59   *Proof! The author resting at 20,000ft (6,000m) on Gauri Sankar.*

When going up, reach up at comfortable arm's length and place one axe into the snow. The nature, direction and angle of your blow/swing will depend on the size and shape of your axe and whether it is inclined or curved. An inclined pick is best hooked into the snow, a curved one best swung. Play at this too. Plant the second axe (or hammer) at roughly the same height as the first and a rough shoulder-width apart. Climb the feet up until shoulders are level with the axes (again roughly – this is an inexact game). Remove one axe, reach up and plant it again at a comfortable arm's length. Curiously it is worth practising the removal of an axe. Some models of axe are notoriously difficult to remove and it is not unknown for climbers to expend more time and energy in removing axes than they did in planting them. If axe removal continues to present a struggle, think about de-tuning the pick as explained in Chapter 1.

There are two accepted ways of holding the wrist loop. In the first, the thumb embraces shaft and loop while in the second the wrist passes clean through the loop and the fist grasps only the axe shaft (*see Figs 20 and 21*). Advocates of the first method say that there is less chance of the heel of the hand slipping from the loop on really steep terrain. Advocates of the second say that it is less tiring on the hand. I prefer the first, but I suspect I'm in the minority. It matters which you decide to use only because the first uses slightly more loop, so that if your hand is in the right place on the shaft of the axe using this method (and the right place is very close to the end of the shaft), it will be uncomfortably off the end of the shaft using the second, unless you shorten the sling. Some axes have adjustable slings which make a change of heart easier, but most of us have knotted our own slings and spent an hour getting the adjustment right. It is worth deciding which suits you better.

THE FRONT-POINTING SEQUENCE (*Fig 61*)

Beginners often grip the axe shaft more tightly than necessary, a common mistake. Hands quickly tire and most of your weight should be taken by the loop around the wrist on the heel of the hand, not by fingers gripping the shaft. Moreover, axes penetrate more effectively if they are held loosely – as you might hold a dart. Whenever possible, allow your feet and legs to take most of your weight. Save your arm strength for the truly vertical sections (rarer than you think, and certainly rarer than it sometimes feels) where body weight is necessarily taken on arms and axes. On these really steep sections, hang by straight arms between placements of the axe – it is less tiring than hanging from a bent and tensioned arm. Efficiency is the key, and efficiency is the only real difference between a good ice climber and a bad one. Some tips in the interests of economy of effort and efficiency are:

1. Use natural holes that sometimes occur in ice – they save a blow of any kind. Simply drop the pick of your axe in and pull down.
2. Take advantage of a recent previous ascent and use the other party's axe holes. This can save a colossal amount of energy and time. For example, this winter on the steep water-ice climbs on Craig y Rhaeadr it was possible to climb entire routes without making a single original axe hole.
3. Practise as great a range of movement on each set of axe placements as possible. The fewer placements and extractions, the

less energy expended. On less than vertical ground it is sometimes possible to mantel over the top of the axe, thereby making more ground per placement. On very steep or vertical ice this will not be possible.

4. Don't grip the shaft – hang on the slings by the heel of the hand.

5. Adjust the axe sling so that you are holding it at the very end of the shaft.

6. If your ice is too soft to hold the pick securely, spin the axe around and use the adze. Terrordactyl and Barracuda adzes are especially good for this. If adzes pull through, try the shaft, slightly above the horizontal. If this fails, go home while you still can; conditions are bad.

7. Change from hooking to daggering wherever the angle allows (below 65 degrees) – it's much faster and less demanding on hands and arms, since you are pushing rather than pulling. The climber in *Figs 61(a)* and *61(b)* has done this, and although he is about to quit daggering, he could well return to it when the angle relents.

In soft snow, the same effect can be achieved by daggering with the shaft instead of the pick. On steep snow, however, this is a precarious and worrying business.

8. Rest aching calves whenever the angle decreases by dropping the knees into the slope, carefully, so as not to disturb the front-points. Rest arms at the same time by allowing them to hang, one at a time if some security is needed, both together if you can stand in balance.

9. Rest badly tiring arms by crooking the elbows into the wrist loop, or by sitting in your axes.

10. Many joules can be consumed in the removal of an axe from a firm lodgement. If your axe is reluctant to part with the ice, try sliding your fist up the shaft and knocking the axe upwards, fist against the underside

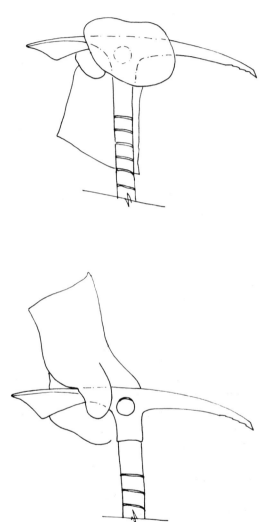

Fig 60 Front-pointing: two ways of holding the axe head when daggering.

of the head. Two or three of these knocks should suffice. Remember to keep the wrist loop around the wrist while doing this, or you'll soon consume more axes than energy.

51

(a)

(b)

(c)

(d)

Fig 61   The front-pointing sequence.

52

(e)

(f)

(g)

(h)

Fig 62 *Economy: a comfortable, balanced front-pointing position.*

Fig 63 *Uneconomical: if you can move this high over your axes it probably means that it is time to think about daggering.*

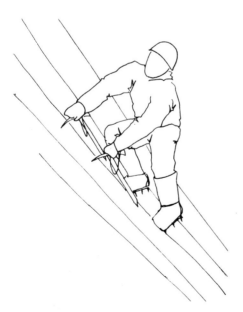

Fig 64 *Daggering and front-pointing is faster and less strenuous than full-blown quadrapedal front-pointing on ground up to 65 degrees.*

Fig 65 *Dave Nicholls daggering on the North Face of the Eiger.*

Fig 66   Roger Mear daggering on Deborah, Alaska.

*Fig 67   Daggering with the shaft in soft, steep snow: Malc Campbell
on Mount Hess, Alaska.*

Traversing (*Fig 68*)

This is awkward when front-pointing. Fortunately most steep snow or ice climbs tend to be straight-up affairs, so the need to traverse is rare. However, it happens (on Zero Gully, for example) and so it is worth a mention. When stretching out to plant an axe as a prelude to a sideways move, don't be tempted into overreaching. An overreach will result in the axe being planted at an angle across the slope with the shaft running towards you. This is fine for pulling sideways, but once you make that move and stand abreast of the axe, you will be pulling directly downwards, which will tend to twist the axe from its lodging. Avoid this by reaching only as far as you can while placing the axe vertically. The inches lost will be more than compensated by the security won.

Descents by front-point are rarer still, and then usually only for very short distances – a move or two. Any greater distance than that will probably merit an abseil – or the discovery of the right route.

(a)   (b)

Fig 68   *Traversing on steep ice.*

More on Front-pointing

There is a faster way to front-point, but I advise it only when you are fairly experienced, and even then only when conditions are good. Instead of placing your axes side by side, and pulling up on them both before reaching up again with one and then the other, place one axe as high up as you can comfortably reach (centrally, for better leverage and balance). Then, pulling up, climb up to roughly nose-to-axe height before placing the second axe or hammer directly above the first one – again as high as is comfortable. If you think about it, this halves the number of times you place your axes on a given pitch. Only attempt this short-cut when you are confident, however – and confident with reason – and when the snow and ice conditions are good.

One final warning: be careful when removing a centrally placed axe. If it comes out suddenly, it may inflict on your face the sort of damage that you have been trying to inflict on the ice.

(c)

(d)

57

MORE ON RESTING
(*Figs 69 to 79*)

Vertical ice makes for strenuous climbing. Make good use of any natural rests – bumps, ledges, shelves, old footholds, everything available. If things get very bad (and sometimes they do) rests may be won in a number of ways. One quick way is to plant the axe, perhaps rather more firmly than you might for a move up, and hook the rope over it, asking your belayer to pull tight immediately you've done so. You can then sit back and enjoy a hand-off rest, contemplating your next move – up or down!

Another method by which a rest may be achieved is to climb with a pre-arranged cowstail (or two if that allows a more relaxing rest). When fatigue calls, plant an axe and clip into it with a karabiner (or fifi hook) whilst hanging from the other arm. This can be reinforced with a second cowstail to a second axe. If you clip into the wrist loops of both axes it will be difficult, though by no means impossible, to slide a wrist back into a wrist loop when you wish

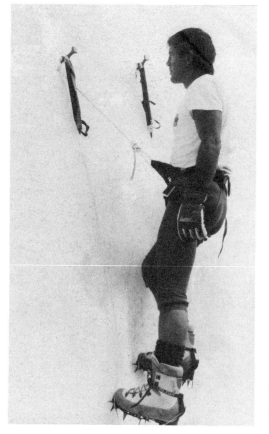

(a)

(b)

Fig 69   *Resting, assisted by a second.*

to resume, because your body weight will be pulling both sides of the loop tightly together. One way of overcoming this is to clip into an entirely separate loop attached to the axe for that very purpose (something more to practise). Another solution is to buy (or make) a wrist loop that has been attached asymmetrically. A clip-in loop is created in the short side so that all your body weight is taken on that side. The longer and un-tensioned side continues to hang open, even when all your weight is suspended from the wrist loop.

Yet another resting method, if you opt to climb with your axes attached to the body with a line or long sling, is to make this attachment of sufficient strength and of the right length, to hang in when a breather is needed. A half rest can be gained by crooking the elbow through the wrist loop (which must be big enough to admit it) and hanging from the elbow rather than hand.

On slightly less than vertical ice (which, nevertheless, *feels* overhanging) it is often possible to stand in balance on your feet. Good climbers will do this unconsciously. In

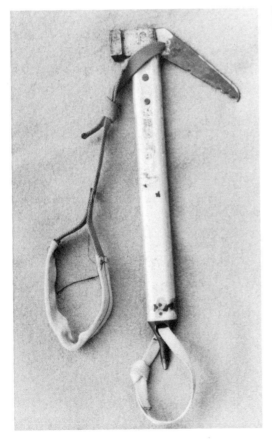

Fig 70 A resting loop which leaves the wrist loop free.

Fig 71 An asymmetrical wrist loop with a sewn-in resting loop.

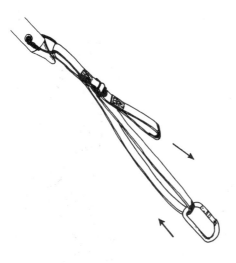

Fig 72 *A more sophisticated resting system: by pulling down on the loop the climber can adjust the length of his attachment to the ice-axe. A thumb under the buckle tab releases the lock.*

(a)

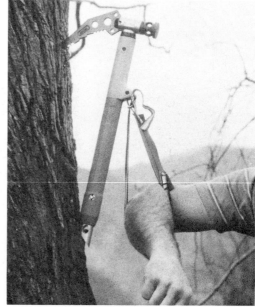

(b)   (c)

Fig 73 *Stubai's adjustable wrist loop in use: (a) the axe is planted, the wrist loop snug to the wrist; (b) opening the wrist loop – a one-handed operation with this particular device; (c) fully opened, with the arm hooked through to rest or to place protection.*

Fig 74   Clipping in to rest.

Fig 75   Resting from cowstails
– though not without betraying
some anxiety.

Fig 76   Note how flat the wrist
loops are being pulled – it will
be difficult to get a hand back
into the right-hand loop
particularly.

Fig 77   Readying to rest from a
long sling.

Fig 78   In this case the sling is
tied via a loop direct to the axe,
not into the wrist loop.

Fig 79   Resting from a crooked
elbow.

any case, never hang on your arms unless absolutely necessary.

As far as I can discover, ice climbing in Great Britain admits to no ethics (I have been careful not to enquire too closely). In North America, hanging on axes for a rest by any of the methods described above, other than elbow crooking, is regarded as using a point of aid – a rather nice distinction which raises the question of what is the purpose of an axe in the first place. It is still regarded as aid when used in order to place a screw. In Britain, no one seems to care how long or often a leader rests or stops in this way to place protection. Perhaps it simply doesn't matter. One of the fine things about snow and ice climbing is that you arrive at the bottom of a route and climb it to the top. There is no preparing of routes by pre-protecting or cleaning. The only cleaning you do is when you're actually engaged in climbing, and then it's carefully in case you clear the bit that's holding you in place. Seems a fairer game to me.

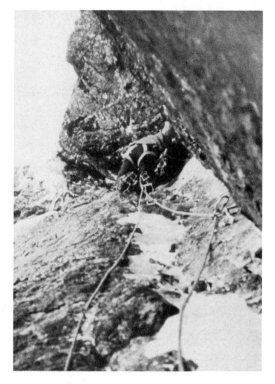

Fig 80   The author on steep mixed ground on Black Cleft (Grade 5/6), Clogwyn d'ur Arddu.

MIXED GROUND, THIN ICE, BAD SNOW

Mixed Ground (*Figs 80 to 83*)

This is ground which consists of rock, ice, snow, earth, turf, and everything in between. Frozen earth and turf work as well as any névé snow. Climbing the stuff is a question of what is available. If there is enough ice – between rocks, in cracks, in patches in the snow – use it for the axe. If not, it may be that you can hook an axe over a rock projection, or wedge or torsion the pick in a crack. Both these ploys are surprisingly secure. If rock predominates, treat it as a rock climb and drop both axes;

they can dangle indefinitely from your wrists while you take by hand whatever is available. Should a chunk of good ice offer itself, flick an axe into the nearest hand and seize that ice.

One hand may be on rock, the other hooking with the axe. The same may be true of your feet. If it is clear that axes will be redundant for some time, it may be more convenient to slot them into holsters, where, in any case, they are quick to hand if needed.

Crampons work well, if noisily, on rock. Climb deliberately, placing feet precisely and searching for flat or incut holds on which to rest the front-points. Practise on a boulder; this is much easier than you might

Fig 81   Discovering what your axe will do on rock.

Fig 82   An axe hooked over a rock projection can be surprisingly secure.

imagine. One consolation on mixed ground is that runners and belays are likely to be better than on pure ice or snow, so don't be dismayed by it. It is as much fun as any other bit of winter climbing, and if it is a little trickier, then it is more rewarding. A bold and positive approach is as good as ten feet climbed.

If you intend to do a lot of mixed routes you may consider doctoring a pair of crampons for that purpose by shortening *all* the points in order to reduce leverage on rock holds and to render them generally more manageable on mixed terrain. In practice, the process of repeated dulling and resharpening will probably shorten the points quickly enough. There are mixed climbs and climbs on snowy rock where old fashioned tricouni nailed boots, or vibram soled boots with a tricouni plate strapped on in lieu of a crampon, will serve better than

crampons.

There comes a time on some routes when the absence of ice and the consequent cacophony from crampons has you wondering whether it is still a winter route. Like everything else in winter climbing, there are no rules, nor even any agreed definitions. The best definition of when a winter route *is* a winter route was given by that eminently sensible fellow Joe Brown when he suggested that if a climb was found to be easier in crampons, it was a winter climb; if not, it wasn't. This is not quite unassailable reasoning, but no one, as far as I know, has managed any better.

Thin Ice (*Figs 84 to 90*)

Unfortunately, ice does not always form in accommodating depth. Rock slabs or walls with as little covering as an inch of ice may

Fig 83 A winter route? The author on the first ascent of a Normandy chalk cliff, one summer's day.

Fig 84 Front-pointing on thin ice: when the ice is this scarce, care is needed not to strike too hard and dislodge what nature has provided. A firm 'nicking' action is required.

Fig 85 Even on ice this thin, the climber (Nigel Shepherd) is able to use his right foot sideways on a small natural ice hold. This rests the calves.

Fig 86 Half a move higher and looking down to see where best to place the feet next, exactly as if he was on rock.

Fig 87 Moving up...

Fig 88 ...again...

Fig 89 ...and again. Note how little of the front-points of the left crampon are penetrating, an indication of how thin the ice is and how effectively well-placed crampons work.

Fig 90 Moving up again on four front-points only.

be encountered. You have a choice which will depend on the thickness and quality of the available ice: either bash it off and climb the rock (if you can), or nick your way up the ice with *great* care and softly, softly.

Bad Snow (*Figs 91 & 92*)

Tom Patey, king of winter mountaineers, is reputed to have said that there is no such thing as bad snow. Maybe not, but there is certainly such a thing as snow that you wish was better. The sort of snow you could find yourself wishing was better might be deep, unconsolidated powder which, contrary to official wisdom, can gather at alarmingly steep angles. The top pitch of Smith's Gully at Creag Meagaidh often holds a twenty-foot (six-metre) section of near-vertical powder. The best approach is the aggressive one. Try for a good runner as close to

yourself as possible and then attack, fight and flounder. Dagger with the axe shafts; even place them horizontally on the end of horizontal arms; a wriggle up, and the same again. Knees, feet and elbows help too. Lurking somewhere underneath it all may be a place for a runner of some sort. Spend some time in search of one. Such powder sections should be short – or you should think about going home until conditions are better.

Deep, wet snow is best left for another day when, with luck, it will have frozen into perfect névé or snow-ice. Wet snow and crampons do not mix well because the snow accumulates under the crampons so that in no time the wearer is standing proud, six inches (fifteen centimetres) higher than usual, and clumping along on feet suddenly pounds heavier. When crampons ball-up like this, hit them sharply with the axe on

Fig 91   The author flounders in powder on Mt Deborah, Alaska.

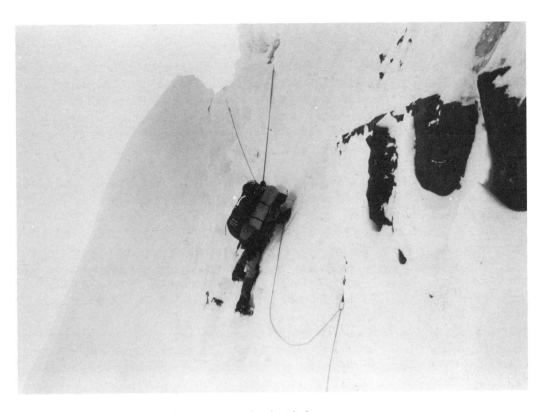

Fig 92 *Steep climbing on powder snow, Mt Deborah, Alaska. Climber: Rob Collister.*

the outside of the offending foot as often as is necessary to keep them clear. This can be done without breaking step, but it takes practice. Better to stop briefly than to stumble.

I have yet to find crampons that don't ball. It is claimed that some are coated with a non-stick surface, but it doesn't work very well. The makers of Footfangs say that they don't ball – they do. Rigid crampons ball more readily than their articulated cousins, but they all ball. Of the various measures recommended to defeat the problem, none, in my experience, are worth the effort. They simply do not work, or they fall apart at the first scrape with mixed ground (for example, wrapping the crampon frame in polythene), or add unacceptable weight to both feet, already heavy enough with big

boots and crampons. This is one of those things that winter mountaineers have to live with.

STEP-CUTTING (*Figs 93 to 95*)

'To cut a step in ice is obviously uncomplicated, and you can fashion it to suit your own taste – soup plates for big feet and mantelshelfing, or "God save all here" jug handles. It is an art form, and self-expression is rare indeed in mountaineering. It only becomes a mountaineering skill when you have the ability to cut a few gross or to do without when there isn't enough ice. However, this approach is only applicable to the historic romantic period which prevailed before the sixties, for the last decade has "done for" the bold, committed leads of bygone days, when the knickerbocker brigade would lead up a hundred feet of ice secured only by a desiccated old ice-axe belay.'

Jimmy Marshall in Mountain

Traditionalists will be dismayed that I have reduced the noble art of step-cutting, once a subject deemed worthy of years of apprenticeship, and deserving of an entire chapter, to a mere section, sulking under a subheading. That I believe to be its proper fate. Climbing moves on. Today's crampons and axes have largely – though by no means wholly – left step-cutting (and step-cutters) to history. For those few times when it is prudent to cut a step, however, it is certainly worth studying how best this is done.

Shallow, though not too shallow, blows are the most efficient. Blows that are too steeply angled merely become embedded in the ice and energy is wasted in extraction. Swing the axe from the shoulder, with a loosely straight arm, rather than from the elbow with a bent arm – the first is much less strenuous and much more efficient.

A step on a steep ice pitch can provide a welcome rest; one foot on is usually enough. Steps will also make an uncomfortable belay stance more amenable.

One little incident illustrates that step-cutting is not dead. On a climb called Central Ice-fall Direct at Craig y Rhaeadr in Llanberis Pass, a veteran and canny climber hesitated below the final icicle which, though very steep and wildly exposed, is short – perhaps ten feet (3m). Where all those who had gone before him that day (it was a perfect Welsh winter Sunday, and a rather busy one) had battered and bruised the poor icicle into submission with mighty displays of strength, our veteran spent a minute chipping half a foothold from one edge of this same icicle. Then he carefully placed his two axes into old holes – he was spoilt for choice – moved deftly up on to his half step, and was up and away before you could wonder at the absence of heaves,

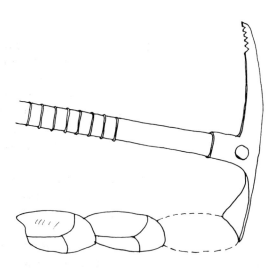

Fig 93   Cutting steps with the adze – always chop away from the first cut.

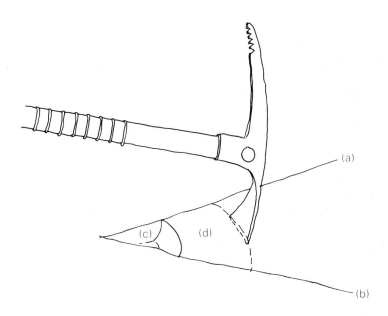

Fig 94 Cutting steps with the pick in slabby snow: make two slashes with the pick, (a) and (b), and then chop between them with the adze, (c) and (d).

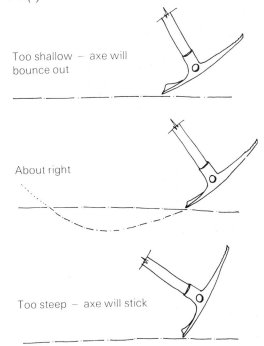

Too shallow — axe will bounce out

About right

Too steep — axe will stick

Fig 95 Achieving the correct angle of attack in step-cutting.

grunts and dislodged ice. So keep some step-cutting arrows in your quiver, and loose them off at those fitting targets.

MOVING TOGETHER
(Fig 96)

Mayhap that you and partner find yourselves on ground where you feel confident that you can dispense with belays (an example might be on short sections of Tower Ridge, under ideal conditions). In these circumstances you might consider moving together to save time, which is of the essence during short winter days. Once it is agreed that this should be done, move off, either with the full 150ft (45m) of rope between you, or, if the terrain makes this cumbersome, a shorter length.

The leader can win protection by weaving in and out of snow and rock outcrops (although this will probably occur, regard-

less of his intention), and by dropping slings over suitable projections as running belays. The second man simply gathers these and returns them to the leader when convenient. Care should be taken by the second to ensure that the rope is kept comfortably taut between them, so that a slip is not further than it need be, and there is no slack to snag or trip on.

SELF-ARREST AND GLISSADING

Some may consider the pairing of self-arrest (or ice-axe braking – I am unsure of which is the more appropriate term) and glissading inappropriate. The pessimists will point out that glissading too often makes self-arrest a

(a)

(b)

(c)

Fig 96   Shortening the rope in three stages: (a) coils taken, each fairly snug under the arm; (b) coils tied off with a figure-of-eight knot; (c) the resultant loop is secured to a karabiner.

necessity, and that glissading is the province of experts. The weakness in this argument is that it admits no way of becoming an expert. The killjoys, and even so joyous a game as winter climbing is burdened with a few, claim that glissading is dangerous and should not be practised at all. Rationally, this argument makes little sense to me, in view of the nature of mountaineering, whilst practically, it disavows a safe and efficient method of losing height – *given the right circumstances*. It is perhaps wise to look at self-arrest first.

Self-arrest, or Ice-axe Braking
(*Figs 97 to 105*)

If you are already a winter hillwalker you will be familiar with this series of skills, and aware of the importance of proficiency in them. Even the most experienced mount-aineers sometimes slip on snow or ice, and a slip can accelerate alarmingly into a wildly out of control fall, especially if the un-fortunate is dressed in smooth-surfaced waterproof clothing, as is likely. To be able to stop, and to stop quickly, is important – sometimes crucial. Under ideal conditions and on gentle slopes the necessary techniques are not too difficult to master. Unfortunately, slips seldom occur under such friendly circumstances, and a tumble on a 30-degree ice slope takes some stopping. As in all things, practice, practice and practice again is the key – and practice early in your ice climbing career. Later may be too late. Choose a concave slope or one with a long, safe run out so that friction will stop you if you fail to stop yourself. Avoid boulders.

In the basic braking position, you lie face to the slope, one hand on the head of the axe with the adze tucked hard in against chest and shoulder and the pick pressed hard to the slope. The other hand holds the axe shaft somewhere near the spike. Some advocate holding the spike itself, so that it cannot pierce the torso if things go wrong. This is worth considering. Hunch the body over the axe. Falls on steep ground will call for all the weight and strength you can muster, so keep your legs splayed for stability, and apply that weight and effort to the pick gradually. Too sudden an effort may result in the pick biting abruptly and the axe being snatched from your grasp. If you are wearing crampons, lift your feet from the snow. If they snag at speed they will cause you to tumble. Don't practise with crampons on – they add unnecessary diffi-culty to an already tricky matter. However, practise as if you were wearing crampons; it breeds good habits.

Fig 97   The braking position, viewed from the snow. The shaded areas show the parts of the body most likely to be in contact with the snow.

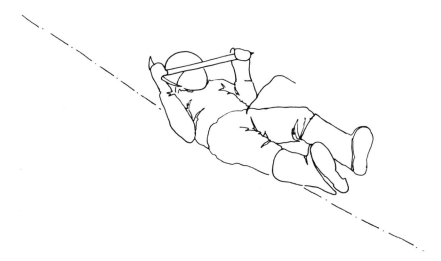

Fig 98   A feet-first fall.

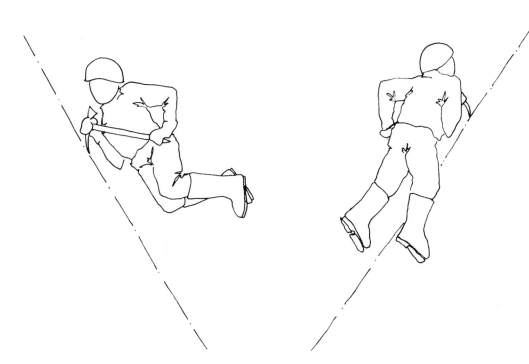

Fig 99   Rolling into the braking position following a feet-first fall. Roll towards the hand that is holding the axe head and apply pressure with the pick gradually so that the axe is not snatched from your grasp.

Fig 100   It is advisable to keep your feet off the snow surface when applying the brake, unless it is very soft snow.

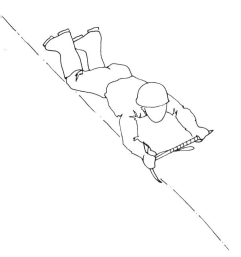

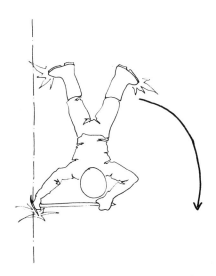

Fig 101   Braking after a head-first fall, face down. Head-first falls are more difficult to control and the first action is to get into a head-uphill position. From here the conventional self-arrest technique can be used.

Fig 102   Falling head-first face down, reach out horizontally with the pick as far as you can on the same side as the arm which is holding the axe head. Bring the pick to the snow and the braking effect on that side will cause your body to swing round past the axe into a head-uphill position.

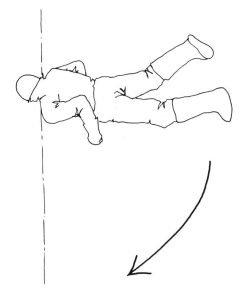

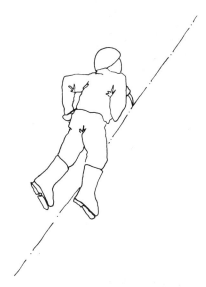

Fig 103   You will now have your arms at full stretch, so arch your back upwards, lift out the pick and place it below your shoulder to brake as before.

Fig 104   The final braking position.

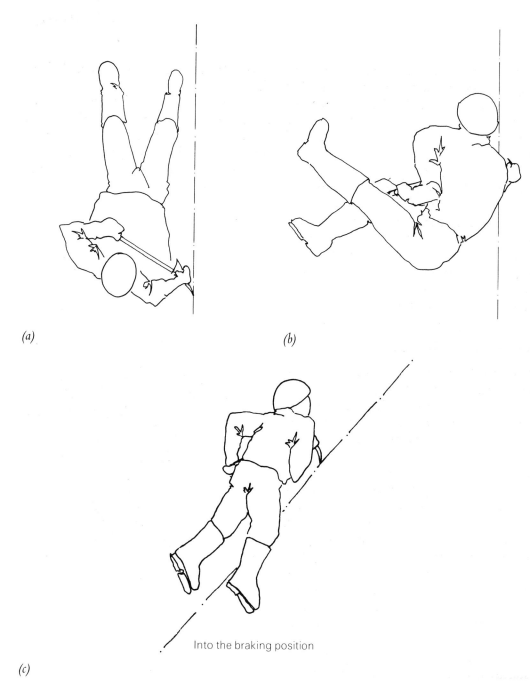

(a)

(b)

Into the braking position

(c)

Fig 105   *A head-first fall on your back: (a) insert the pick close to your hip and on the same side as the arm which is holding the axe head. (b) Dig the pick in and at the same time pull yourself into a sitting position. (c) Bring your knees up towards your chest, then swing your legs away from the axe head and allow them to fall through into a position with your head uphill, from which a normal arrest can be made.*

Should you find yourself tumbling after a slip, spread-eagle with arms and legs. This will stop the tumble. Then apply the braking technique appropriate to the attitude in which you find yourself post-tumble.

Rucksack and crampons, both of which you are likely to be wearing when a real fall occurs, serve to complicate matters. Since, in my own experience at any rate, real falls are always much faster and more furious than practice falls, it behoves you to invest some hours in self-arrest. The skill and effort needed to stop a slide should not be taken lightly. Speed of reaction may be vital.

Glissading (*Figs 106 to 111*)

Glissading is enormous fun and a very quick and efficient way of losing height. It can, however, be dangerous. Common sense is the key. There are two methods: standing and sitting. The standing glissade is the harder to perfect, but probably the more comfortable once mastered.

The position and execution of a standing glissade are akin to those of skiing, although your skis are only as long as your feet. Position the body as far forward as is necessary to keep your weight directly over your feet, which should be flat on the snow. Keep your feet comfortably apart and parallel, hands wide for balance, and axe at the ready for a self-arrest, should your glissading fail to convey you to the bottom of the slope with the grace of a thousand startled gazelles. Turn simply by turning the feet whilst keeping the weight over the outside/lower foot, just the same as skiing.

The sitting glissade's only advantage is that you are closer to the slope when a fall does occur. It is no easier to perform and will almost certainly lead very quickly to a

straightforward (and very practical) bum slide.

Quite why the bum slide should be the subject of such opprobrium in the eyes of 'professional' mountaineers, instructors, guides and the like is not clear. It is a safe, speedy and foolproof way to descend – *under the right circumstances*.

Fig 106   A standing glissade is performed in a skiing position.

Fig 107   A standing glissade, albeit a wobbly one!

Fig 108   A bum slide.

Fig 109   A bum slide off the Pic Sans Nom. Bum slider: Tim Jepson.

Fig 110   A standing glissade; the axe is at the ready should it be needed.

Fig 111   The bum slide; axe at the ready, crampons off. Waterproof trousers improve both slide and comfort.

And the right circumstances, as with glissading are:

1. It is safer on a slope that you know, or that you can see the bottom of. The slope should also be avalanche and obstacle (boulder) free. A good run out forgives errors.

2. Watch out for changes in surface texture – soft snow to ice will result in dramatic acceleration.
3. Stay in control.
4. Keep your axe at the ready as a brake.
5. Expect some wear to the seat of your pants – and possibly your backside as well!

3 Belaying and Protection

A CAUTIONARY TALE

'An easy snow slope led up to the foot of the gully which in turn led easily for a hundred feet to the first steepening. Here we uncoiled the rope, tied on and sorted out some gear. As Scrim scratched about for a belay, my attention was caught by a scraping higher up. Looking up I saw the backside of a climber about to disappear up and over a bulge fifty feet above. He was generating a fair flurry of snow and I thought it would make a good photograph – bum and flying snow against the blue of the sky. As I focussed, he zoomed in. He'd fallen off. He'd landed on me. He'd embraced me; stuck fast. Fortunately Scrim had me tight on belay a split second before or I think we, the "bum" and I, would have quickstepped a downwards dance. A shout! Again I looked up. There, plucked clean as a goose down from rock and, presumably, belay by the "bum's" tight rope, was his partner, stark against the blue sky and a good way towards it. But he came down, crashing down; plucked such a twang that he passed over us, some way out, and skidded to a landing on the easy snow slope beneath. One hundred and fifty feet beneath. But not to a stop – which is what saved him. He skidded on, decelerating imperceptibly, what Scrim later called the "Holmenkollen effect" (after an Olympic ski-jump near Oslo over which, Scrim claimed, a mate had slid on a tin tray – to a new world record). As the lower man skidded, the rope between him and "bum" stretched its full elastic stretch. "Bum" looked at Scrim; held on to me. Scrim shrugged at "bum"; held on to me. Good and tight please Scrim.

Scrim held fast. I held fast. The other fellow clung with drowning puppy eyes. Oh those eyes, the things they said! Twang. Whang. "Bum" was off again, torn from our grasp. And so they travelled, yo-yo, full three hundred more feet until a scoop stopped them. They lay inert, surely dead. I untied and ran down. They were stirring, groaning. I, dreading the inspection – the damage surely in bends, breaks, holes, rips, tears – arrived, it must have been only thirty seconds later, hardly daring to look. They were standing, feeling, squeezing, easing, brushing; miraculously unhurt; speaking!

"Eh," said the one, a Yorkshire lad, "I wish I could get the hang of this front-pointin'".

"By," said the other, also a Yorkshire lad, "but that were exciting".'

This incident, from my book *The Great Climbing Adventure*, took place not many years ago in Twisting Gully at Stob Coire nan Lochan, Glencoe. It illustrates the less than satisfactory fact that when climbing on snow and ice, a falling climber all too often means two falling climbers. It should not be this way, nor need it be, and on the whole, levity notwithstanding, I would prefer to have been spared that tumultuous fall.

All other things being equal, a rock belay is to be preferred to an anchor in snow or ice (I have assumed that you are acquainted with the mechanics of belaying on rock which will not be described here; I am concerned only with winter modifications to the general practice). It may come as some comfort to learn, in one of those curious, inexplicable little ethical quirks that help to make climbing such a fascinating game, that the use of pitons, unsanctioned on a summer rock climb, is perfectly acceptable on a winter route. Your rack of chocks and nuts (pared for winter use) is therefore likely to include a small selection of pitons. If you have been a purist all your rock climbing days, you will need to get some experience as to how these pegs work. Practise on a remote boulder, where no one is going to be offended.

If, however, no rock belay is available despite an hour's exploration and excavation – and that is frequently the case – what to do?

BELAYING ON SNOW

The methods available, each best suited to different circumstances and conditions, are:

1. Ice-axe.
2. Deadman.
3. Snow bollard.
4. Foot-brake.

Ice-axe Belays (*Figs 112 to 118*)

Horizontal (buried) axe: properly constructed, this is a good method of belaying. Some important considerations when using this type of belay are:

1. The buried axe should be lying against the near (to the belayer) shoulder of the slot.
2. Don't disturb the integrity of the snow around the slot – it contributes greatly to the holding power.
3. The same method can be strengthened

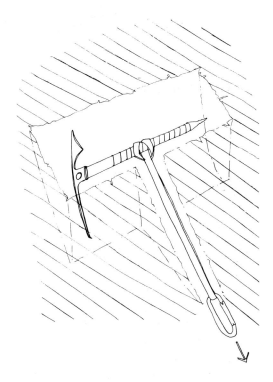

Fig 112   A belay on to a buried horizontal axe.

with the addition of a second axe: the reinforced axe, or 'T' axe belay. A generally less satisfactory variation is shown in *Fig 114*.

The combined working surface area in a 'T' axe belay, with average length axes, is about the same as that of a deadman – and it is easier to set up correctly.

Vertical axe: modern axes with metal or glassfibre shafts are certainly strong enough to take the load generated by the holding of a fall. In the right circumstances, an axe placed vertically in the snow can be used as a belay anchor. This method should only be used where the result of a slip is likely to be a slide, rather than a clean fall, and when the

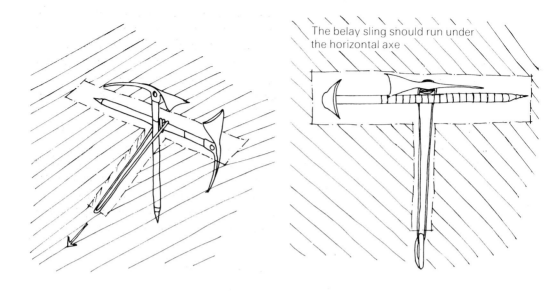

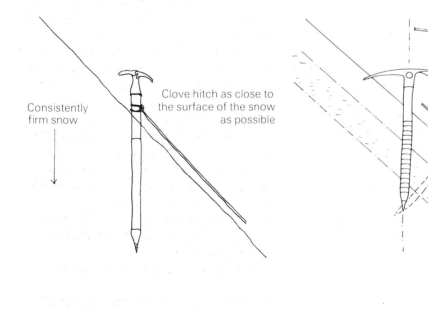

Fig 113   A reinforced or 'T' axe belay.

Fig 114   A variation on the reinforced or 'T' axe belay.

Fig 115   A vertical axe belay.

Fig 116   A vertical axe in the wrong circumstances; be wary of layers of varying hardnesses.

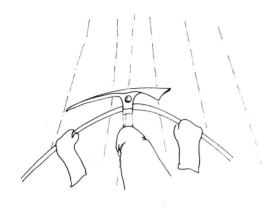

Fig 118   A direct belay on to the ice-axe shaft.

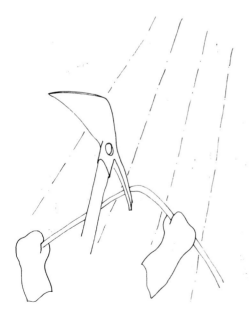

Fig 117   A direct belay on to the pick.

snow is hard enough to require the axe to be hammered in. Softer snow will not hold the axe firmly enough. Failing light and poor weather may also justify this method on the grounds of increased speed – although security should not be compromised too readily.

Two methods of using the axe for a direct belay (direct from the second to the anchor) are shown in *Figs 117* and *118*. Again, these should only be used in the right circumstances, for example, when faced with a short, steep step whilst moving together across otherwise easy ground on good névé.

Deadman Belay
(*Figs 119 to 123*)

The deadman (not the happiest of names) has been around for fifteen years or so. It is known as a fluke in the USA and Canada, the saying being 'it's a fluke if it works'. It is a spade-shaped alloy plate with a wire strop through centrally located holes. The idea is that the plate is embedded in snow in such a way, and at such an angle, that any pull on it will only bury it deeper and any move – if it moves at all – will increase its security. A well-sited deadman will work in most sorts of snow, powder being the only certain exception. A disadvantage of the deadman is that the angles of correct placement are fairly critical and the top of the Ben on a wild winter day is not the best, or the easiest, place to guess exactly what is 50 degrees. Like everything else, siting a deadman is worth practising.

The deadman is 'planted' as follows:

1.   Cut a T-shaped slot, with the bar of the 'T' across the slope, disturbing as little of the surrounding snow as possible.

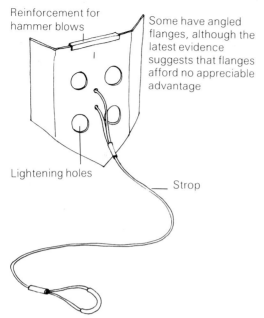

Reinforcement for hammer blows

Some have angled flanges, although the latest evidence suggests that flanges afford no appreciable advantage

Lightening holes

Strop

Fig 119   A deadman.

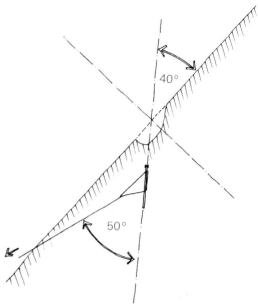

40°

50°

Fig 120   The correct angles for placement of a deadman.

2.   Insert the deadman at an angle of 40 degrees to the upper snow slope. This angle is most easily discovered by resting the shaft of an axe perpendicular to the slope (giving an angle of 90 degrees). Bisect it with the deadman, and tilt the deadman back a smidgen (precisely a 5-degree smidgen) and push and hammer it home to a depth of a foot or so. If loose snow lies above a hard layer it is best to clear that loose snow away, exposing the firm underlayer. Check too that the deadman is not apparently firmly bedded in a layer of firm snow that is lying on a layer of even harder snow. The lower, harder layer will provide a good sliding surface for the upper, softer layer, and a slide may be triggered by a pull on the deadman. A general alertness in the course of the climb will supply this sort of information.

3.   The vertical stroke of the 'T' accommo-dates the wire strop. Ensure that this is sufficiently deep (scraped clear with the pick of the axe) to avoid self-ejection. Insuffici-ently deep slots are the main cause of dead-man failure. A bump left in the slot will act as a fulcrum when the wire is drawn taut over, it, and the resultant force sends the deadman skywards with alarming ease.

When you are happy that the deadman is correctly positioned, clip your climbing rope into the loop at the end of the strop with a karabiner and descend to the site of your stance. You should position yourself far enough below the deadman to ensure that the rope from it to your waist/harness is pulling the plate in the right direction – downwards, with no hint of outwards. In practice this always means going further down the slope (usually with some reluct-

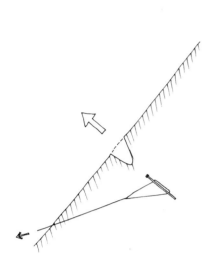

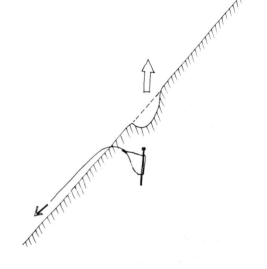

Fig 121   Incorrect deadman placement.

Fig 122   Incorrect deadman placement.

ance since it will have recently cost you energy in the climbing) than you initially imagine is necessary. This could be as much as 10–15ft (about 3–4.5m), depending on whether you intend to stand or sit to belay. The shallower the angle of the slope, the further from the deadman it will be necessary to belay in order to ensure a downwards, as opposed to an outwards, pull. A moment's thought will make the reason for this clear. The internal angle between wire and plate should not exceed 50 degrees. This is hard to judge, not least because the plate is buried and so it is better to over-insure: go lower. There is no reason why a sling can't be clipped to the deadman strop and a belay taken on the sling, except that in practice this often results in a stance too close to the deadman and a bad angle between strop and deadman. Using the rope gives you far

greater freedom than a sling, or even several slings.

Some winter climbs, and many on Ben Nevis, finish on flat ground. Good belays can be hard to come by in such places. You will be tempted just to go well back, sit down, and take a waist belay without an anchor. In practice this is often a perfectly satisfactory thing to do – though do go *well* back. However, a deadman works well in horizontal terrain too – the same guidelines apply. Expect to place the deadman as much as 30–40ft (9–12m) back from the lip, especially if there is a cornice to avoid.

Think about the snow. If it has good natural cohesion (old snow, windslab, névé), disturb it as little as possible. If the snow lacks cohesion (powder, wet snow, porridge) then the area can be stamped solid before placing the deadman.

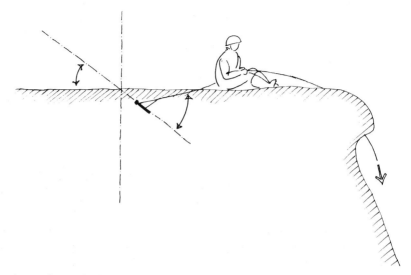

Fig 123   Belaying from a deadman on the horizontal.

Snow Bollard (*Figs 124 to 127*)

For years I held, in ignorance, that the snow bollard belonged to the category 'tricks for instructors'. I was very wrong and have since used them 'in anger' the world over, although always for abseiling. But the principle is the same when belaying.

The diameter of the bollard is governed by the hardness of the snow: it may need to be as much as 10ft (3m) in soft snow. The channel along and around which the rope passes needs to be deep enough to avoid the risk of the rope riding up – and out. The rope will tend to 'cheese wire' into the bollard which can be reinforced with rucksacks, spare clothing and axes. (We used the rubbish we were dutifully carrying off the mountain on one occasion in Alaska – the desire to live being greater than our collective environmental conscience.) In layered snow, have the rope encircling the stoutest layers. Sit well below the bollard.

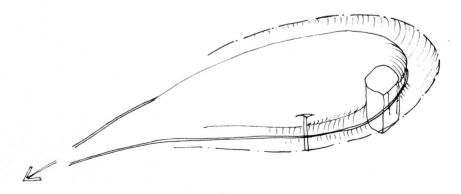

Fig 124   A snow bollard should be reinforced with clothing and rucksacks.

Fig 125   Abseiling in earnest from a snow bollard (though it is difficult to see) on Deborah, Alaska.

Fig 126   A snow bollard belay.

Fig127   *Abseiling from a snow bollard. Note that the climber has strengthened the wall of the bollard with an axe. This would be removed by the last man once the team are satisfied that their creation will bear the strain.*

Foot-brake
or Boot-axe Belay (*Fig 128*)

This technique is reputed to have been imported from New Zealand and is a handy method for use by a party, who, moving together, encounter a tricky step on otherwise straightforward ground (the sort of place where you might also consider using a vertical axe belay). It works well only when done well. In soft snow the boot braces the top of the axe, as well as offering friction to the rope. This friction may be increased by wrapping the rope back around the heel of the bracing foot. Such a belay, and a cool head, will cope adequately only with slips and slides: don't ask too much of it.

In soft snow

In hard snow brace the axe against the lower leg

Fig 128   *The foot-brake.*

BELAYING ON ICE

The methods available are:

1. Ice-screws.
2. Ice bollards.
3. Threaded icicles.

Ice-screws (*Figs 129 to 136*)

Some ice-screws are solid, others hollow; some are driven in and screwed out, others screwed both in and out. None are perfect and none work in all ice conditions. Only experience will tell which to use where and

when. In the right conditions ice-screws make adequate anchors for belays and running belays, but the right conditions are fairly rare. They may, however, be all there is available – especially on steep water-ice climbs.

To place a screw-in ice-screw:

1. Clear away rotten ice and any snow cover.
2. Cut a small starter hole – two or three blows with the pick should suffice.
3. Tap the screw gently and begin screwing by hand.
4. Screw by hand and then by axe pick if

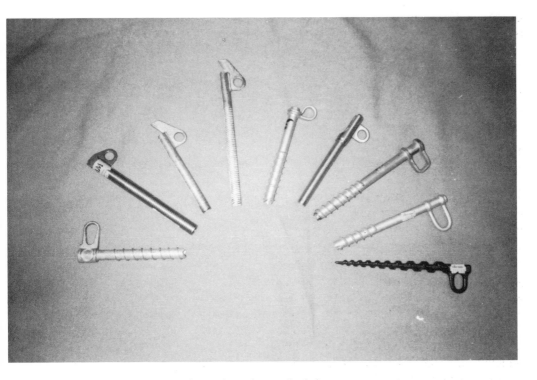

Fig 129   A selection of ice-screws (left to right): Chouinard tubular (screw-in, screw-out); D M M ice tube (drive-in, screw-out); Lowe – Camp Snarg; Lowe – Camp Snarg; Salewa tubular (the most recent design); Salewa Snarg; Salewa tubular; Camp tubular; Salewa Warthog (solid, drive-in, screw-out).

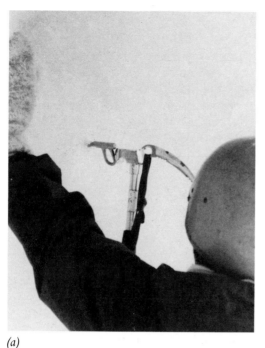

(a)

(b)

Fig 130   Two ice pegs being driven home: (a) a Warthog (drive-in, screw-out); (b) a Snarg (tubular, drive-in, screw-out).

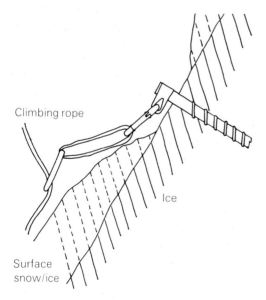

Fig 131   An ice-screw correctly placed and clipped to the climbing rope via a sling. Note: snow or poor qulaity surface ice has been cleared before insertion.

greater leverage is needed, at an angle perpendicular to the ice or 10 degrees above it. Continue to screw until the lug or ring at the head of the screw is flush with the surface. This may mean cutting away a few bumps. If the ice is not deep enough to accept its full length, the screw should be tied off with tape, at the junction of screw and ice, to reduce leverage.

Some screws, notably those made by Chouinard, are so well designed that they can be both started and then screwed for their entire length by hand alone. 'Drive-ins' are simpler to place – rather like driving a household nail. They are, however, more likely to damage the ice into which they are being driven because the ice they displace has to be compressed into that surrounding the drive-in. This causes 'starring', especially in brittle ice. Tubular screws like the

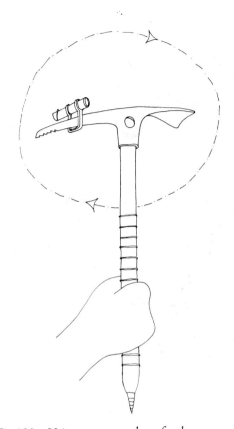

Fig 132   Using an axe as a lever for the insertion or extraction of an ice-screw. Note: on insertion, it is usually possible to turn by hand for about half the length of the screw; on extraction, the axe is usually only needed as a lever for the first few turns, after which it should be possible to unscrew by hand.

Chouinard (screw in, screw out) or Snargs (drive in, screw out), are less likely to star ice because the ice they displace is extruded up the inside of the screw and emerges at the head in a core. They impose less pressure on surrounding ice than solid drive-in pitons.

Further points to note when inserting ice-screws are:

1.   If you intend to belay to ice-screws, use two (or more) and place them at least a foot (30cm) apart.

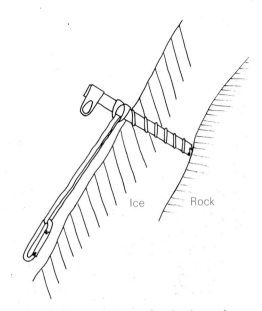

Ice   Rock

Fig 133   This screw, having foundered on rock, has been tied off to reduce leverage.

2.   The colder the ice, the more solid will be the screw. They freeze in place.

3.   Screws conduct heat, so if the sun gets at the heads they will melt out in no time. Where there is no shade the heads can be covered (with snow, gloves, hat, etc.).

4.   Long screws hold better than short ones provided that they are fully in. Tie off screws that project more than half an inch above the surface.

5.   Once a tubular screw has been used it may be blocked with ice. It will not work in this condition. Before re-use either clear the ice with a drive-in or carry the tubular screw inside your jacket where body heat will perform the same job, albeit at some discomfort to yourself.

6.   If an ice-screw that you are inserting bottoms on rock, do not attempt to screw it deeper – and be alert to the possibility of this happening. A further turn is likely to result in a spectacular 'dinner-plate' and a blunt screw. Better to leave the screw where it is and tie it off, or try again in nearby ice.

93

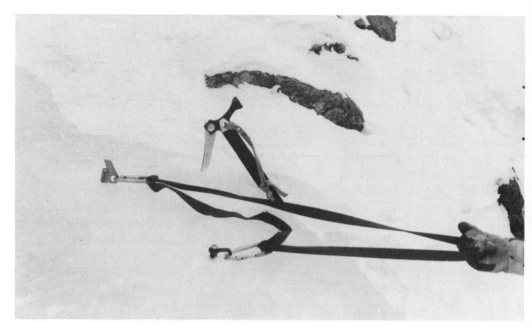

Fig 134 Belaying from two ice pegs: a snarg on the belayer's right; a Salewa tubular screw in the centre. They are a good foot (30cm) apart and tied off independently with one long sling by means of clove hitches.

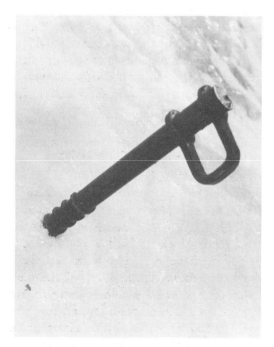

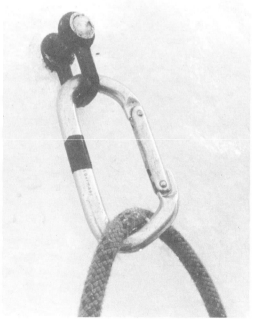

Fig 135 Starting a screw.

Fig 136 A properly placed screw.

7. If a screw stars or dinner-plates, take it out and try again nearby.

8. Chouinard sells a ratchet which greatly speeds screwing and unscrewing and I have seen climbers toting conventional ratchet spanners adapted for use on screws.

9. Screws will work in water-ice and some hard snow-ices. Treat all with suspicion and learn by experience what textures and colours of ice take them best. A perfect screw will hold up to 4,400lb (2,000kg).

Ice Bollard (*Figs 137 & 138*)

This works on exactly the same principle as a snow bollard, but ice, being a stronger substance, allows a smaller version – as little as a foot (30cm) in diameter in solid ice. Ice bollards are indisputably stronger than even the best placed screws, but they take time and some energy to fashion, factors which do nothing for their popularity. In escape they are good to abseil from, especially since no gear need be left behind. Sometimes

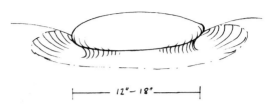

Fig 138   An ice bollard.

nature provides a half-formed one in just the right place. The hand of man may put the finishing touches to it, but be prepared to leave well alone. That final cut in the pursuit of artistic perfection is all too often the blow that decapitates. Or look what happened to De Milo's Venus!

Threaded Icicles

On water-ice climbs, nature sometimes supplies threads around icicles or at the junction of two naturally formed holes. If these threads look strong, use them. There is no ready way of assessing their strength, so they ought only to be used as a secondary anchor unless there is nothing better, in which case try to arrange at least an ice-screw in support.

A NOTE ON BELAYING
(*Figs 139 to 141*)

Whenever belaying in snow it is worth spending a minute seating your backside comfortably deep and kicking your feet into good buckets. All this will enable you to hold a fall more efficiently, make it less likely that you will be jolted from your stance, and allow you to take much of the load on your body before any load is transmitted to the belay anchors themselves. The last is a particularly good thing when the belay

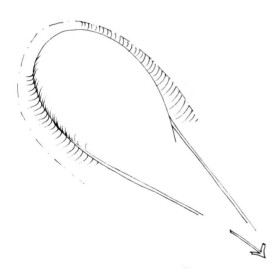

Fig 137   An ice bollard (oblique view).

Fig 139   *Prepare a good stance (the rucksack needs a berth too).*

Fig 140   *The stance; stamp your feet in well and seat your backside firmly.*

anchors are not above suspicion; on occasion, this may be an inescapable circumstance. Whilst ideal for rock climbing, belay plates can be troublesome in winter conditions with frozen ropes, ice encrustations, etc. That is not to say that they can't be used. Many, however, dispense with them in winter and revert to the waist belay. If this is how you decide to belay there is a further safety consideration: if your rope is tied into the front of your harness from where it runs straight to the belay anchor, you will be in danger of being spun around in the event of holding a fall. This could leave you facing into the mountain with the leader falling behind and below you, opening your arms and making it almost impossible for you to do anything about it.

One answer is to tie off at the rear of the harness, as shown in *Fig 141*. This is slightly more awkward to complete than the conventional belay plate arrangement, but is much safer – as your leader is likely to agree. The integrity of a waist belay may further be improved by passing the rope from the controlling hand to the leader through a karabiner clipped into the *front* of the harness. This ensures that whenever a leader travels above you, whether to left or right, the rope always passes through the front of your harness and cannot be pulled away from that place whatever happens subsequent to a leader's fall. In ideal circumstances I would recommend that both these modifications are applied. If time, circumstance or laziness counsel otherwise, then at

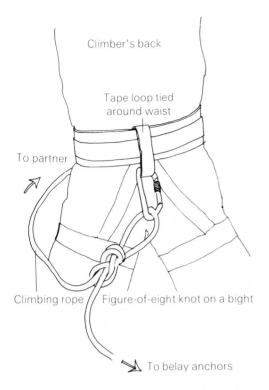

Climber's back

Tape loop tied
around waist

To partner

Climbing rope   Figure-of-eight knot on a bight

To belay anchors

Fig 141   Tying off at the rear.

least employ the second modification. I urge this in the light of realism: it doesn't resolve all possible contingencies, but it is the easier and, therefore, the more likely to be applied. If, for some reason, you cannot tie off at the back of your harness before belaying and rely instead on an arrangement whereby you belay directly from the anchors to the front of your harness, you can at least ensure that the rope used to tie the belay and the line rope – that is the rope running from your hands to your partner – both lie on the same side of your waist. This precaution will render an unsatisfactory method much less unsatisfactory, and it is neither difficult nor time consuming.

If you elect to climb in a waist belt, rather than in a harness, you will be able to swivel

the assembly around your waist to your back, so achieving rather more simply the same effect as that shown in *Fig 141*. There is an argument, and a reasonable one it is, which claims that, for winter use, a waist belay is to be preferred to a belay plate. The reasoning here is that while arrest in the case of the plate will be sudden – and therefore violent – the waist belayer can always allow some rope to run through his gloved hands as he stops the fall. Arrest in the latter case will be more gradual, less violent, and safer. Leaders, or at least falling (or fallen) leaders, can be forgiven if they are less than wholly enthusiastic in their support of this argument. But the fact is that whereas on rock the sooner a fall is stopped the better, on snow (or ice), where a fall may mean not much more than a steep slide down a gully, albeit a fast and furious one, concern about the strength of the anchors might reasonably outweigh concern for the victim's immediate welfare. It all very much depends on the precise circumstances at the time and upon such considerations as the shape and topography of the climb.

RUNNING BELAYS
(Figs 142 to 144)

Again the dictum 'rock belays best' applies, and running belays in or on rock are nearly always better than their ice counterparts. The more, the better principle applies too – within reason – though the tendency on steep ice is to use fewer runners than you might in the same distance on a rock climb. There are probably two reasons for this:

1.   It takes some effort and time to place a screw, particularly if there is no resting place from which to do the job. In this case the

Fig 142   One method of freeing the hands to place screws for running belays on steep ice.

Fig 143   An alternative way of freeing the hands.

Fig 144   An icicle provides John Cousins with a good thread runner on The Wand (Grade 5), Creag Meagaidh.

climber will have to hang in his axe by arm or sling, a performance which persuades most that a screw about every 10–12ft (3–3.5m) on very steep ice is sufficient.

2.   Some climbers develop such confidence in their axes that they regard them as hand-held, mobile runners and their confidence produces long, fast, runnerless run outs – and sometimes longer, faster falls.

In perfect Scottish snow/ice conditions, most of us will feel secure enough to be able to dispense with our rock climbing quota of runners. In the absence of ethical pressure, the rule is: use as many as you like, but as few as you are happy with.

As on rock, natural spikes and bollards will sometimes occur. Use them. Icicles too sometimes present good threads, as can trees or bushes in some areas.

4 Starting Out

'We shall go
Always a little further: it may be
Beyond that last blue mountain barred
   with snow.'
            'Hassan', James Elroy Flecker

'Mountaineering is a struggle and winter mountaineering often a desperate one. No dry exercise of logic and skill, but a "Hawking of immense jug handles", a frozen waiting in icy torrents of "thundering rubbish"; a fight with the rockless wastes of the last 400 feet of Scotland while the sinister dark clutches at your ankles, a world where to spend time is maybe to spend your last time, and where only the bold stroke will suffice, where victory is celebrated not with a shaming glow of smugness but with great baying whoops of triumph and relief, a world of primitive delight.'
            Robin Campbell in *Mountain*

FIRST WINTER ROUTES

Suitable advice as to what sort of winter climb you should choose for your début depends pretty much on the rock climbing experience you have so far garnered, which is not to say that you have to rock climb before you turn to winter routes. That is usually the way of it, but I can think of no good reason why a first ever climb shouldn't be on snow or ice. An E6 climber should have little difficulty with most Grade 3s, although no winter route is ever a waste of time and even the ascent of a Grade 1 'snow plod' will add to the receptive mountain-

eer's well of experience. If you are happier on Difficult or Very Difficult rock you are still likely to be able to hack a winter Grade 3, but it might be that something easier is more to your liking to begin with. It is arguable that there is little correlation between summer rock and winter ice ability. There are E5 rock athletes who shiver at the thought of Grade 5s ice, and modest Very Difficult rock climbers who dispense with Grade 5 in fiendish style. I suggest that you start with something easy anyway – you can always go looking for something harder next time.

But what kind of route? Gullies are nearly always great fun if conditions are reasonable, that is, not too warm and not too much soft snow. Some gullies are long – over 1,500ft (450m) – although not necessarily, indeed seldom, of sustained difficulty throughout. It might be a good idea to start on something shorter or something on which the difficulties are known to be short-lived.

Ridges give tremendous sport in almost all conditions, although bear in mind that once a start has been made, there may be no easy escape from even the most straightforward of ridges. Poor snow conditions need not be a crucial factor as long as the foot of the ridge can be reached safely. Wind could be a hazard, though; gusts can be uncommonly strong, in Scotland especially. I have seen big heavy men brought literally to hands and knees in a by no means freak Glencoe howler.

Buttresses and iced rock tend to produce the hardest winter routes and their difficulty, sometimes even their feasibility, will frequently depend on the amount of ice they have been blessed with that winter (which is in some part true of all manner of winter routes).

Frozen waterfalls and waterweeps are either there (or as mountaineers say, 'in'), in which case they can be climbed, or they are not, in which case there is no climb to be contemplated. Tradition insists that they are graded. I can never see the point. Look at a waterfall: you can see how long it is, how steep it is; feel how plastic is the ice and make up your mind, after a reconnaissance, whether or not it's for you. The grade will vary wildly from year to year according to the depth of the ice, the temperature and how many teams have been there before you. (But I won't stand any longer in the face of tradition.)

My advice for absolute beginners would be take it easy at first – there are years ahead of you – and have some respect for the wildness of winter weather. Ask for advice about local conditions; play at it before getting too serious; and don't worry too much about going home empty-handed. For those who want to know how enjoyable a wild winter climb can be, I have included an essay about a foray in Raven's Gully on Buchaille Etive which I hope serves as a taster (*see* Appendix).

GRADES (*see also page 128*)

There are a number of different grading systems in current use throughout the world. The Scottish system shown here is the most widely accepted and is used throughout Britain. A winter grade is the roughest of assessments, for while the length of a climb will scarcely vary (although entire pitches sometimes sink without trace), just about every other factor affecting the difficulty of a climb can – and almost certainly will – change.

Grade 1: Uniform, low angled snow or ice slopes. Unlikely to be steeper than 50 degrees.
Grade 2: Steeper, longer slopes, with perhaps a step or two of rock, ice or snow.
Grade 3: Climbs of any length and steepness usually characterised by ice bulges which, though not sustained, may be approaching the vertical; easy waterfalls; some ridges, for example Tower Ridge.
Grade 4: Hard climbs with sustained sections of steep ice; steep buttresses; steep waterfalls.
Grade 5: Long, hard climbs with difficulties of all kinds; long, steep waterfalls; difficult buttresses and ridges.
Grade 6: Anything considered abnormally hard for a 5.

There is some debate about the merit and necessity of Grade 6. On balance I think that the Grade 6 has earned its right to stay, if only to protect the upwardly mobile Grade 5 from being stretched to the point of meaninglessness. When I climbed Black Cleft one winter I decided that if Point Five was a Grade 5, Black Cleft must be a 7, which may or may not be true, but it does show that the grading of winter climbs is little better than random.

GUIDE BOOKS

Guide books for almost every British and American winter climbing area are usually available at climbing retailers, especially for areas local to the retailer. A guide is a wise, almost essential investment and good ones make good reading for pub, café, hut, tent, or belay – if your partner is slow or lost – or bivouac, if you're both slow or lost!

Few North American ice climbing areas have guide books yet, but they are beginning to appear. Meanwhile, the journals usually describe those areas where the hot climbers are hanging out. Again, refer to the nearest climbing shop for local information.

MAPS

A map of the area in which you intend to climb is as good an investment as a guide book (1:25,000 is best; 1:50,000 will do very well). Not only will it give the guide book an extra dimension, but it will often get you home, with a little help from a compass, when nothing else will. Navigation in winter is trickier than in summer – streams and small lakes may be concealed from view – so take time, take care, and take a map and compass.

If you are trying to find your way off a corniced plateau (such as Ben Nevis or Creag Meagaidh) in a white-out, beware of navigating by following the line of the plateau edge, and, if you are in any doubt as to your whereabouts, remain roped. Furthermore, you might consider pitching it – yes even on the flat!

Fig 145   The plateau summit of Ben Nevis.

THE CLIMB

Where and When; There and Back

There is good winter climbing to be found in all three countries of mainland Britain, and even westerly, wet Ireland sports one or two once in every other decade. Scotland, however, owns by far the greatest number and variety of climbs: the Northern Highlands (Beinn Bhan, Beinn Dearg, The Fannicks, Torridon); Ben Nevis; Glencoe; Creag Meagaidh; and the Cairngorms. North Wales at its best is as good as most of the Scottish areas, but dons its full winter raiment for little more than a week or so, and even then not every year. (The winter of 1986, and the month of February in particular, was an exception.) Nevertheless, it's the rare winter in North Wales when something, somewhere, doesn't come into 'nick' - an elusiveness that will often fill the evening pubs with armies of discontented weekenders. The Lake District too boasts some first-class winter climbing, but even less often than Wales. So Scotland rules in quantity and reliability. Quality is a matter of opinion (and some heated debate), but good is good whether north or south of the border, or east or west of Offa's Dyke.

Chapter 6 provides suggested areas, classic routes, and how-to-get-there information. This 'starter kit' in no way replaces a guide book, but it might whet your appetite. It should also remove some of the enshrouding mystery that seemed to veil the whole game when I started and found myself floundering up the wrong side of the Ben in search of a route!

All the areas that I have listed (and some more) are well served by guide books which provide the newcomer with sufficient information to make that first foray not too much of an adventure. A lengthy browse of the appropriate guide is recommended, as time spent in reconnaissance is seldom wasted (*see* Further Reading for most of the guide books currently available for winter climbing in Britain). Apart from details of routes and their length and grade, the guide will give other useful, perhaps vital, information, of which the way off the climb is as important as any. For example, there are three or four good ways off Ben Nevis, but none of them absolutely straightforward in poor visibility and one that, although easy in fine weather, demands good compass work and some accurate dead reckoning in bad. I'd be prepared to bet that more accidents have occurred on the Ben in winter on easy ways down than on difficult ways up. Part of the problem in Scotland is that so many of the climbs end on almost featureless plateaux – as you will discover for yourself on the Ben, at Creag Meagaidh, at Lochnagar and in the Cairngorms. It is difficult to overstate the importance of knowing the way off your climb.

When?

The British winter climbing season is about as definitive, reliable and trustworthy as a party political broadcast. Point Five Gully, one of the Ben's great climbs, has been climbed in perfect conditions as early as November and as late as June. The most consistently good conditions throughout Britain (which are still pretty inconsistent) are found in the months of January, February and March. February is arguably the best, with lengthening days, an accumulation of snow and still fairly cold.

It is probably worth telephoning to check conditions before embarking on a northwards marathon. You may have inside information, or you could ring a National Centre (Plas y Brenin in Wales, or Glenmore Lodge in Scotland) or somewhere like Nevisports in Fort William. They will be happy to help.

Getting to the Bottom

Wales has short walks in, the Lakes longer, Scotland longest. Be prepared for anything up to a three-hour flounder in a Scottish bog, and only a slightly shorter walk out. Plastic boots and over-gaiters are about the only things, outside an unusually solid freeze, that will get you to your climb with dry feet north of the border. The scale of things makes for long, tiring days. Be good to yourself; be fit, start early and try not to finish the climb too late – winter days are short.

As you approach the route, be aware of the snow conditions and if they are manifestly poor, consider an alternative – a ridge perhaps, or a day profitably spent playing on an ice boulder. Winter climbing is an increasingly popular game and a late start can mean, amongst other things, a miserable day under a fusillade of falling ice – the discharge of which not even the most delicate of front-pointers seem to avoid. Few need to be coaxed to wear a helmet; few need to be convinced that they are *de rigueur*.

Once in a blue moon, it is possible to ski into winter routes. These blue moons occur slightly more often in Scotland than elsewhere in Britain. Most modern ski-mountaineering bindings will fit (or can be made to fit) plastic boots. One of the very best days I ever had in British hills was when Roger Mear and I skied from the boot of our car in the Spittal of Glen Muick car park all the way up to Lochnagar, passing a dozen foot sloggers on the way – and all this

stripped to the waist in brilliant sunshine. We climbed Parallel Gully B in perfect conditions and skied back to the boot of the car by moonlight, a magic day. (Roger went on, though not immediately, to ski to the South Pole.)

Tooling Up

Don crampons early rather than late. On the Ben, for instance, in an averagely snowy winter, many put on their crampons as low as the CIC hut, a full hour short of most of the routes. On most winter routes it is best to carry your rucksack on the route. This is likely to contain spare clothing, food, a first-aid kit, some spare crampon nuts and screws (and strap, if appropriate), a Swiss army knife or a screwdriver, a crampon spanner, a flask with a hot drink perhaps, a spare pair of gloves or mitts, goggles, a poly bag large enough to accommodate a body before it becomes a 'body', map and compass, whistle and your climbing gear. All this results in a heavier sack than any of us like to carry, but anything less should be given wary consideration. There are winter climbs, many of those in Cwm Idwal in Wales for example, where rucksacks can be safely and sensibly left at the foot of the route to be collected, not much later, on the way down.

Carriage and Management of Gear

'Now, with technological ravages typical of the modern mind, you can hardly get near the ice for the mass of gear to be carried – staves, screws, deadmen, curving pick hammers, axes, whistles, pieces, clinometers, etc. Second men would be better trained as caddies, or building Yosemite

Fig 146 The mass of gear to be carried.

prams to trail up the ice walls. This is possibly "sour grapes", for I also carry some of these items, but confess to finding them singularly useless!'

Jimmy Marshall in *Mountain*

Of all the accoutrements with which the 'modern mind' has burdened the modern ice climber, the deadman is the most awkward to carry. Indeed, it is difficult to see how it

could be more awkward. I suggest one of two methods:

1. Join the two ends of the wire strap with a karabiner and carry it over one shoulder like a sling.
2. A more convenient method, though slightly more time consuming, is to wrap the strap around the deadman until only the end loop remains. Tuck this through a lightening hole or through the rest of the strap and attach it to your harness, at side or rear, with a karabiner. Some models of deadman have two locating slots on either side of the plate for just such a purpose. If yours doesn't, the same effect can be achieved by intertwining the strap through the lightening holes until only the end loop remains.

I have mates, whose opinion I value, who have given up trying to make a deadman swing about the body and have relegated the instrument to a home on the outside of the rucksack, from where, they claim, they can deploy it as quickly as from anywhere else.

Once upon a time there were, in addition to deadmen, deadboys and dead babies. These offspring are (fortunately) now considered to be too small to be effective and have been allowed to die a natural death.

But deadmen apart, the scope for becoming snarled up in your own gear is tremendous, with your headlamp cord, helmet straps, balaclava ties, hood toggles, ice-axe slings, rucksack straps, hip-belts, zippers, crampon straps, gaiter laces, and climbing rope. Two things are certain: at some stage you will tangle with some of your jangling gear, and never – well, hardly ever – will any of it be as conveniently to hand as the situation seems to demand.

How best to carry gear is a controversial subject, but clearly something must be

Fig 147   A deadman, coiled for carriage.

attempted. You have five choices: carry it in your harness (waist or chest); or on a bandoleer; or on a combination of both; or in the shoulder straps of your rucksack; or even in the rucksack itself. The last option is surprisingly popular and singularly useless. Any one of the first four methods may suit you, so think about it and experiment. A tidy system may save hours on a long route and those saved hours may save the route –

and all sorts of horrors besides.

If you elect to carry your gear slung from the harness, grass skirt-style, as you might on a summer rock climb, take care that it doesn't dangle too close to your crampons on the way down. I know of very good climbers who have broken world descent records, launched unwittingly to stardom, if not starwards, by snagging a crampon point on a favourite runner.

I leave the last word on the subject to Harold Raeburn:

'Think of everything you could possibly want on a climbing expedition, say, of thirty hours. Cut out from this all that you think might be fairly easily dispensed with. Take with you 50 per cent of the remainder.'

On reflection, it is probably better to take too much and prune with experience. And too much will certainly include a deadman, four or five ice pegs of one sort or another, a selection of nuts, some slings, karabiners and, perhaps, a friend or two.

CLIMBING CONDITIONS

Weather

'What would the world be, one bereft
Of wet and of wildness?'
Gerard Manley Hopkins

British winter climbs are often conducted in appalling weather of the sort that, anywhere else in the world, would send most of us scuttling for shelter. Indeed Harold Raeburn, Scottish pioneer extraordinaire, talked with relish of 'full conditions' – a blizzard – as if anything less than ferocious was cheating. Sunny or snowy, welcoming or wild – great days can be had in winter almost (but not quite) regardless of the weather. I once met Yvonne Chouinard, doyen of American ice, in a café in Fort William. He had just failed on Zero Gully in a thaw.

'Man, how can you climb that stuff?', he complained. That night it froze hard and the next day he romped up in fine style.

'Man, how can you grade that stuff?', he

Fig 148   The author trying to ignore the weather.

wondered.

Despite Raeburn, and despite a long tradition of ignoring the weather almost to the point of foolhardiness, the weather, and the snow conditions it governs, do matter. Scottish winter weather is described in technical terms as Polar and in less prosaic terms as ferocious. The full fury of a wild winter day is not to be underestimated.

A thaw, especially one that rises above

3,000ft (900m) or so, is bad news. Wet snow is no fun to climb, wet ice may fall, wet cornices become heavy, droop and drop. Then it will be very dangerous in the gullies; less so on ridges and buttresses. Deep, new powder can be fun, especially on ridge and buttress, but in heavy accumulations it can also make any gully a dangerous place. Spindrift might be considered part of the game, but if it is too heavy, or prolonged, you may care to think again. A freeze following powder only serves to prolong its existence, but a freeze following a thaw produces that finest of Scottish ice, something between white ice and snow-ice, perhaps unique to the wet, cold British Isles, and a joy to climb; akin to polystyrene, someone said. Fortunately, the thaw/freeze cycle is a common one.

Weather forecasts are available from radio, newspapers, TV, some RAF stations, National Mountain Centres at Plas y Brenin, Capel Curig, Snowdonia, Wales and Glenmore Lodge, Aviemore, Cairngorms, Scotland, some climbing shops, and telephone weather services. It should not be difficult to secure a forecast and it is always worth trying, even if forecasting is an imprecise science. I feel that having a little knowledge of the weather is a classic case of:

'A little learning is a dang'rous thing;
Drink deep, or taste not the Pierian
  spring
There shallow draughts intoxicate the
  brain,
And drinking largely sobers us again.'

If you wish to drink deeper, in order to know more of it than its immediate effect on your climbing day, a number of publications are given in Further Reading.

Snow and Ice

Snow can be roughly categorised in order of hardness, from snow to powder snow, to packed snow, to névé (firm and hard after the thaw/freeze cycle), to white ice or snow-ice, to blue/green ice, to black ice (for example old, worn, couloir ice). Alternatively, beginning as liquid, it changes from water, to water-ice, to blue/green ice (if it grows old enough).

Anything from névé and harder is good to climb on, although blue ice is hard work, work that a cold day makes harder still. A warmer day, however, will make blue ice easier because the surface will have softened to admit pick and front-point. Warm ice, that is just above or just below zero, is plastic; cold ice is brittle, the colder, the more so.

Experience will teach at which colour of snow or ice it is best to aim your axe. The differences in shade and texture in both snow and ice are fairly subtle, but knowing about them can save hundreds of calories, hours, and sometimes the day. The firmness of snow is seldom uniform across its entire surface, so learn what colour is the good stuff. Ice is more consistent but it will still betray good and bad spots to the enquiring climber (grey and opaque patches are often good).

Retreat

Sometimes we have to give the mountain best. Escape is not always easy. Look for abseils from existing pegs (check them first), or from spikes, or from snow or ice bollards.

Cornices

Some easy climbs are capped by insurmountable cornices. Sometimes they can be dodged to one side. Other times they have to be tunnelled – often a long and tiring performance. There are those who claim to enjoy such antics.

In thaw conditions, avoid gullies that display a cornice. Beware the snow slope immediately below a cornice, as it is nearly always the site of a quantity of windslab, a substance not unlike névé to sight and touch (though duller in the sun), but dangerously unstable to boot and axe. Cornices can grow to prodigious size, the Scottish variety especially – don't underestimate them or the inconvenience they represent.

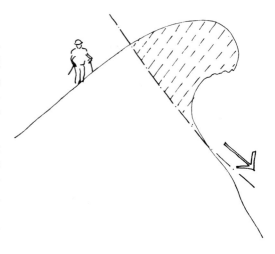

Fig 150   The probable sheer line of a cornice.

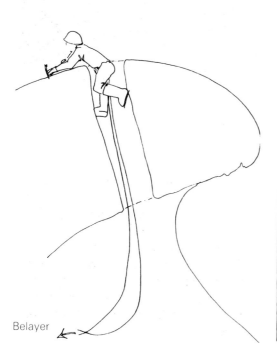

Belayer

Fig 149   Cornice tunnelling.

Fig 151   A bigger than average cornice. Karl Tobin takes a look at a monster on the East Ridge of Deborah, Alaska.

Fig 152   Emerging from a small cornice at the top of S.C. Gully (Grade 3), Stob Coire Nan Lochan. The belay is of the 'how not to' variety.

BENIGHTMENT

The combination of long walks in, long climbs, and short days will sometimes benight even the speediest of climbers. Be watchful of the time, there is merit in speed, and, if you have to spend the night out, spend it as comfortably as possible. Spare clothes, a piece of Karrimat for the backside, some food, a headlamp, and a repertoire of songs and yarns will all help. In his classic essay, 'Tower Ridge Rule Book' (in *Cold Climbs*), Robin Campbell gives us this gem as Rule Six:

'Don't under any circumstances decide to spend the night up there (Tower Gap) and finish your climb in the morning. This luxury from the heady days of German Romanticism is no longer available. The local Mountain Rescue team will be up in a flash, buzzing round with dogs and helicopters, and you won't get a wink of sleep. Not a wink. Press on and take your chances.'

Perhaps it is better not to be benighted. If you are, and there is sufficient snow, you can use it to build a shelter.

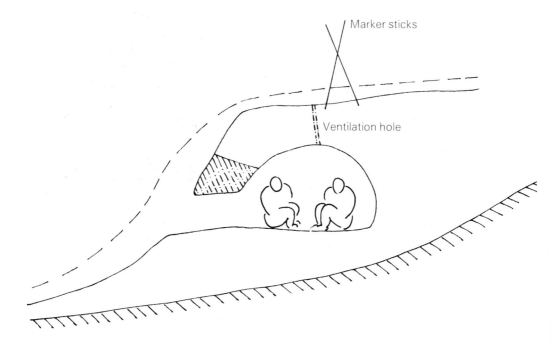

Fig 153   *Section through a simple snow cave dug into a drift.*

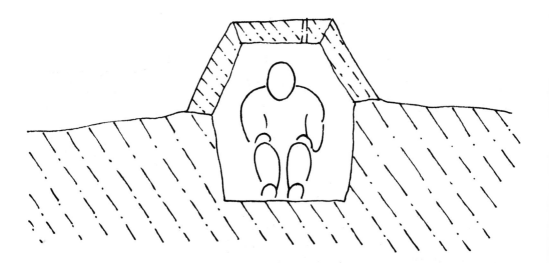

Fig 154   *A snow coffin – a simple emergency snow shelter made by digging a shallow trench and laying slabs at angles against each other as a roof.*

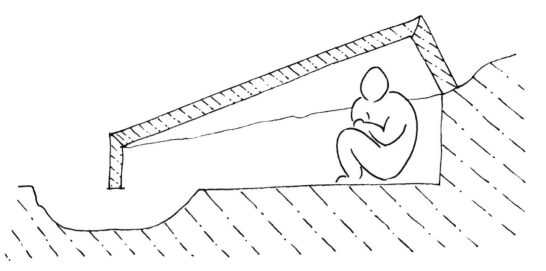

Fig 155   Section through a snow coffin.

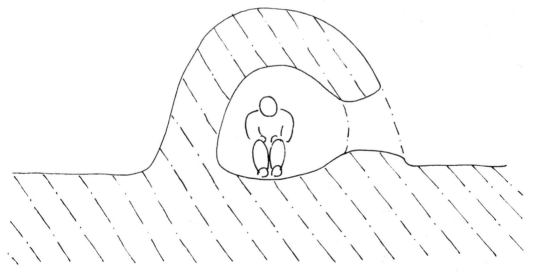

*Fig 156   A shovel-up snow shelter. This type of shelter can be
constructed from only a few inches of snow. Collect snow by shovelling it
into a mound about 10–12ft (3–3.6m) in diameter and 6ft (1.8m)
high. Allow the mound to settle – the drier the snow, the longer this
will take. Dig into the centre via a door-sized hole and throw the snow
thus excavated on to the top of the mound. This principle will work with
all types of snow; wet snow can be dug out immediately, powder snow
may take an hour to consolidate.*

Fig 157   Snow holes on Ben Nevis.

TRAINING

Training days in the winter hills of Britain are often long and tiring – as long and tiring as many a fully-fledged Alpine day. It pays to be fit enough to enjoy the walk home afterwards. Running for training will take care of that. As far as climbing is concerned, anything less than vertical should not prove too exhausting if tackled with a degree of economy and with some semblance of technique. Climbing vertical ice, however, is undeniably strenuous, even for those with the most svelte of styles. In general, the stronger you are the better you will fare. Weight-training, pull-ups – indeed, anything that strengthens the hands and arms – will help to turn desperation into competence, if not nonchalance. I know an American who has constructed a frame in his back garden, over which, every winter, he splashes water, via a hose, from the kitchen tap. The result, once frozen, is a 30ft (9m) high ice tower (a height greater than that would require planning permission). If that seems a little extreme, trees make very good

Fig 158   No need to wait for snow or ice for practice sessions...

Fig 159   Trees make very good surrogate ice climbs.

surrogate ice climbs, pliant softwood being as climbworthy as the very best névé, if a little sensitive environmentally. Chalk cliffs too work well with axes and crampons most of the time, although there are those who would have us believe that chalk cliff climbing is a game in its own right.

5 Winter Hazards

AVALANCHES

It comes as a surprise to many newcomers to winter climbing that avalanches are a common occurrence in British hills. Almost every year climbers are swept to their deaths by avalanches, while a greater number are injured by them. Scotland, with its greater accumulation of snow, suffers most, but Wales and the Lake District know avalanches too. (A curious and macabre fact is that the greatest number of deaths occasioned by an avalanche in Britain occurred on the Sussex Downs in 1836.)

Like weather forecasting, the assessment of avalanche risk is an imprecise science. No one, it seems, understands the phenomenon perfectly. Indeed, some of the most knowledgeable avalanche experts have themselves been victims.

A number of very good books have been written on the subject (*see* Further Reading). I recommend a thorough scan of them. They are all very readable and you need not be a scientist to enjoy or understand them. Whether or not a slope will avalanche depends on a complicated sum of a number of interacting factors: temperature, surfaces, snow depth, wind, angle, gravity, past weather, and probably a few more. You must at least recognise the fact that avalanches occur in British hills every winter, and know in what circumstances they most readily happen, what types of avalanche are most common, and how to avoid them in the first place.

When?

In theory, an avalanche can happen on any slope above 18 degrees or so. More common angles, however, are between 30 degrees and 50 degrees. Above 50 degrees they are rare because snow seldom accumulates in sufficient depth on a slope of that steepness. Any snow slope or gully is potentially prone to avalanches. Dangerous times are:

1. When it is snowing heavily (a rate of 1in (2.5cm) an hour is considered heavy in this context).
2. Two or three days after heavy snow.
3. During thaws (wet snow slides and cornices falling).
4. *Any period when wind and snow have coincided* (including wind-driven, old snow).

Avalanche Types

For the mountaineer's purpose, there are two broad divisions of avalanches: loose and slab. A loose snow avalanche has little internal cohesion and moves in a formless mass, beginning at a single point, in wet or dry snow, and broadening as it gathers momentum. Loose dry snow moves more quickly but is less imprisoning than loose wet snow, which slides slowly but weighs heavily on a victim. The latter is the more common loose snow avalanche in Scotland, thanks to frequently wet weather.

Slab avalanches occur when an area of windslab snow (that is, snow that has been compacted by the wind) breaks away in a blanket, leaving a clearly defined fracture

Fig 160   A slab avalanche.

line. On the mountainside the climber is often both trigger and victim. The slab so released varies from yards to acres square, and is characterised by internal cohesion. Windslab is that snow deposited on the *lee* slope when wind and snow combine. That this can occur during snowfall will be obvious, but don't forget that snow, being a loose, mobile substance, can be blown about *after* it has ceased to snow. When this happens, it may be by a new wind from a different direction – beware. It can be packed surprisingly hard (variations in the strength characteristics of snow are among the widest found in nature: the hardness of wind-packed snow may be 50,000 times that of light powder snow). It can also be deceptively hard, giving the appearance and feel of névé. Be suspicious. It is betrayed by a matt surface and exploration with an axe will soon reveal its slab nature. Treat all lee slopes with circumspection, particularly after long periods of winds prevailing from a particular direction. After days of westerlies, for example, many of the east facing slopes on Creag Meagaidh will be slab avalanche prone. As has already been explained, the area immediately beneath a

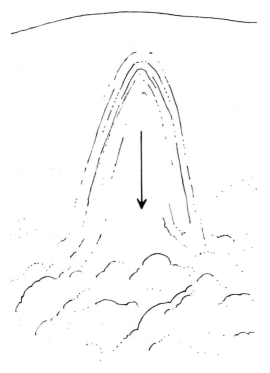

Fig 161   A loose avalanche.

cornice (a wind-formed feature) will often consist of windslabbed snow. Of the two broad types, slab avalanches are the more dangerous because they are less predictable and better disguised.

AVOIDING AVALANCHES

Reading Ground

Steep gullies (the line of the majority of winter routes) and open snow slopes are natural avalanche paths. Ridges, outcrops and terraces are natural avalanche barriers. Ridges are always the safest place in terrain prone to avalanches. If, for instance, it has been snowing heavily for two days and you

are determined to bag a route, try to make it a ridge or a buttress. On the Ben, Castle Ridge, Tower Ridge and North East Buttress might well provide superb alternatives to any gully or face climb that you originally had in mind. (There are those who maintain that Tower Ridge and North East Buttress are the best routes on the Ben in the first place!) Better advice, though, is not to climb at all until the new snow has had time to settle – one or two days at least.

Rock outcrops are islands of safety. Rough, irregular ground tends to hold back slides, at least until the irregularities have been filled in and smoothed over with snow. Smooth ground, or ground on which grass is lying flattened, offer good sliding slopes to just a few inches of snow.

The avalanche potential of a given slope usually recedes with time – until it snows again.

Safety Points

1.   Whenever practical, expose only one member of the team at a time. The other might well be belayed at the side of a gully or to a rock outcrop.
2.   Try to steer clear of the avalanche paths.
3.   Don't stop or rest under an avalanche path.
4.   Avoid times of greatest danger, that is, during or immediately after snowfall of more than 1in (2.5cm) an hour, or after prolonged periods of high wind.
5.   Be aware of the temperature: the colder it is, the longer new snow remains dangerous. Common sense tells us, however, that new, wet snow followed by a severe frost will quickly produce stable, safe and superb climbing conditions.
6.   Beware lee areas and especially those below cornices.

7. Keep to gully sides and walls.
8. Cross potential avalanche slopes as high as possible, hugging the foot of any buttresses.
9. If you must climb on an avalanche slope:
    (a) Close up your clothing, don hat and mitts and raise your hood (all of these actions increase your chances of survival if buried).
    (b) Loosen rucksack straps so that it can be jettisoned if necessary.
    (c) Climb directly up or down, rather than across, when possible.
    (d) You might consider trailing an avalanche cord from your belt. There is a chance that an inch or two of it will remain on the surface, even though you are buried.
    (e) Take advantage of any protection that nature has provided, such as rock outcrops or ridges.

Notes for Victims

If you are caught in an avalanche:

1. Call out so that other members of your party can watch your course in case you are buried.
2. Try to delay your departure. In a small slide you may be able to plant an axe and hang on long enough to avoid being swept away. Even if you are carried away, the longer you can delay, the less snow there will be to follow you and to bury you.
3. Discard your rucksack.
4. Attempt, with a swimming motion, to stay on the surface. Try to work to one side of the moving snow. In a large or fast-moving avalanche these efforts will probably be of little avail, but they may save your life in a smaller one.
5. If you find these efforts are not helping,

cover your face with your hands. This will help keep snow out of your nose and mouth, and you will have a chance to clear a breathing space if you are buried. Avalanche snow often becomes very hard as soon as it stops moving. You may not be able to move your arms once the snow has stopped.
6. If you are buried, try not to panic. Frantic and fruitless efforts to free yourself consume valuable oxygen. Stern self-control is essential to survival.
7. In soft snow you may be able to dig yourself out, or at least make room to breathe. Make sure you dig upwards, towards the surface. Avalanche victims sometimes lose their sense of direction and try to dig down.
8. If you hear rescuers working above you, don't waste your strength by shouting. Though sound transmits *into* snow easily, it transmits *out* poorly.

Notes for Survivors

1. *Don't panic* – the lives of your buried mates may depend on what you do in the next hour. Check for further slide danger and pick a safe escape route in case of a repeat avalanche.
2. Mark the last point where victims were seen on the avalanche path. This will narrow the area of your search and that of the rescue party. Use an ice-axe, rucksack, rope, or clothing as a marker.
3. Make a quick search. If there are only two or three survivors, they must make a quick but careful search of the avalanche area before going for help. If at all possible, one survivor should be left to continue the search and guide the rescue party.
4. Search the surface below the last point where the victim was seen for evidence of him or clues to his whereabouts. Mark the

117

position of any pieces of equipment you may find – these will provide clues as to the victim's path. Search carefully and kick up the snow to uncover anything which may lie just beneath the surface.

5. If you are the sole survivor, you must still make a thorough search of the avalanche before going for help. This may seem obvious, but it is a rule all too often neglected. Even the simplest search may enable you to find the victim and free him alive.

6. If a rescue party can be summoned only after several hours or longer, which in Scotland is likely to be the case, the survivors must concentrate on making as thorough a search as possible with their own resources. The chances of a buried victim being recovered alive diminish rapidly after two hours.

7. If the initial search fails, begin probing with your axe. Trees, ledges, benches or other terrain features which have caught the snow are the most likely places. If there are several survivors, probing at likely spots can continue until a rescue party arrives. If you are alone, you will have to decide when to break off the search and seek help.

8. Send for help. If there are several survivors, send only two. The remaining survivors must search for the victim in the meantime. If it will take two hours or more for help to reach the scene, and the avalanche is not too large, the victim may have a better chance if everyone remains to search. This is a difficult decision to make, and depends on circumstances.

9. The rescue party will normally expect you to guide them back to the accident scene unless its location is absolutely clear.

10. If the victim is found, treat him immediately for suffocation and shock. Free his nose and mouth of snow and administer mouth-to-mouth respiration if necessary. Clean snow from the inside of his clothing and place him in a sleeping bag, with his head downhill. The very gentle application of external heat will help counteract severe chilling. Any further injuries should then be treated according to standard first-aid practices.

A summary of action to take is:

1. *Check for further danger.*
2. *Mark last point seen.*
3. *Quick search.*
4. *Thorough search.*
5. *Send for help.*

FROST-BITE

The following text on cold injuries has largely been culled from *Medicine for Mountaineering*, edited by Professor James A. Wilkerson MD.

The climate on Britain's winter hills can be Polar. Frost-bite, though not common, may catch the unwary or unprepared. Frost-bite is an injury that is caused by cold sufficient to freeze tissue. The hands and feet, which are furthest from the heart and have tenuous blood supply, and the face and ears, which are usually the most exposed portions of the body, are the areas most commonly involved.

The principal effect of cold is to impair the circulation of blood to the affected area. When the body is chilled, the blood vessels in the skin contract, particularly in the extremities, reducing the amount of heat lost by radiation into the surrounding atmosphere. Thus, body heat is conserved at the expense of lowering the skin temperature.

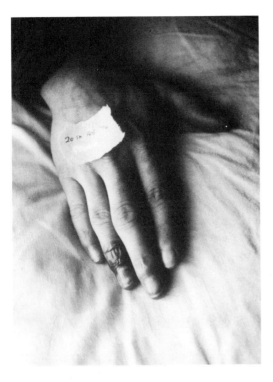

Fig 162   A bad case of frost-bite, Scotland 1974.

Under these circumstances, blood vessel constriction may become so severe in areas which are more severely chilled that circulation almost totally ceases.

As the circulation is impaired, all sensation of cold or pain is lost. Unless the tissue is rewarmed promptly, the skin and superficial tissues actually begin to freeze. With continued chilling the frozen area enlarges and deepens. Ice crystals form between the cells, and then grow by extracting water from within the cells. The tissues may be injured physically by the ice crystals.

Prevention

Frost-bite can occur in any cold environment, but is usually associated with an overall body heat deficit resulting from inadequate clothing or equipment, reduced food consumption, exhaustion, injury, or a combination of these factors. 'Wind chill', rather than purely temperature, determines the rate of heat loss.

Heat production, from exercise or the protective mechanism of shivering, is just as important as clothing in maintaining body temperature. Often the second, belaying a leader on a long pitch, is the one who suffers frost-bite. An accident victim lying immobilised may suffer frost-bite even though he appears to be more than adequately clothed.

Insufficient food and exhaustion can reduce the body's store of nutrients to a level at which the body temperature can no longer be maintained. Under these circumstances, relatively minor injuries may produce shock which predisposes the victim to cold injuries.

The earliest signs of frost-bite are a sensation of cold or pain and a waxy white pallor of the skin in the affected area. As freezing progresses, the tissues become even whiter and all sensation is lost. With deep frost-bite the tissues become quite hard.

During and following thawing, the injured area is often extremely painful. One to three days after thawing the site of injury appears red and is severely blistered – first with small blebs and later with large, coalescing blisters. In more severe injuries, or when rewarming has not been properly performed, the tissue has a dull, ashen grey colour. Later it may turn black and appear dried and shrivelled. Appearance, however, often suggests a much more severe injury than actually exists. Even mild cases of frost-bite look frightening if blistering occurs.

Treatment

In recent years most of the older methods of treatment for frost-bite have been shown to be ineffective or even harmful. Rubbing the injured area or massaging with snow – both were once thought to be effective – only increases the injury. A frozen nose or ears can be rewarmed with a hand held gently against them. Frozen fingers and hands can be rewarmed in armpits or crutch. Feet may need a sleeping bag or the inside of a good friend's jacket. If spotted early enough 'frost-nipped' extremities can be rewarmed on the hill. Warmth, colour and sensation will return, leaving a very superficial injury. In such cases, it will probably be safe to continue. If recognition, and therefore treatment, is delayed and the freezing is deeper, seek qualified medical advice as soon as possible. Treatment of frost-bite is a job for an expert.

An individual who has suffered frost-bite once is more susceptible to subsequent cold injury because the blood vessels in the injured area are damaged permanently. It's worth looking after yourself.

MOUNTAIN HYPOTHERMIA

A decrease in core body temperature to a level at which normal muscular and cerebral functions are impaired is known as hypothermia. Normal body temperature is within one degree of 98.6 degrees Fahrenheit (37 degrees Celsius). A wet, cold, windy environment removes body heat rapidly. Exposed skin is the most important source of heat loss by radiation, convection, evaporation, and conduction. Heat loss from an uncovered head or bare hands may account for as much as fifty per cent of the total body heat loss at air temperatures below 40 degrees Fahrenheit. Dry clothing traps a layer of warm air which is an efficient insulator. The high thermal conductivity of water (over 200 times that of air) greatly reduces the protective value of clothing when it becomes wet.

Heat loss, especially from wet skin, is greatly increased by wind. 'Wind chill' is an important factor in increasing the chances of cold injury or hypothermia. *Fig 163* summarises its effect.

Heavy physical exercise increases heat loss by increasing evaporation from the lungs and sweating, which also deplete body fluids. Exercise in a cold environment requires more energy and a higher water intake than equivalent exercise in a warm environment.

In a survey of eight cases of hypothermia in Britain, of which five were fatal, the following causes were present:

1. Bad weather – setting out in extreme weather conditions or being overtaken by bad weather, especially blizzards.
2. Being benighted – more cases occurred in individuals who pushed on to exhaustion than in those who bivouacked.
3. Being wet or having insufficient clothing – inadequate protection against wind, not least over the *lower half* of the body – was a common feature.
4. Exhaustion – physical exhaustion was a contributing factor in the more serious cases.
5. Inexperience and lack of training.

Prevention

Awareness of the causes of hypothermia and the rapidity with which fatal hypothermia

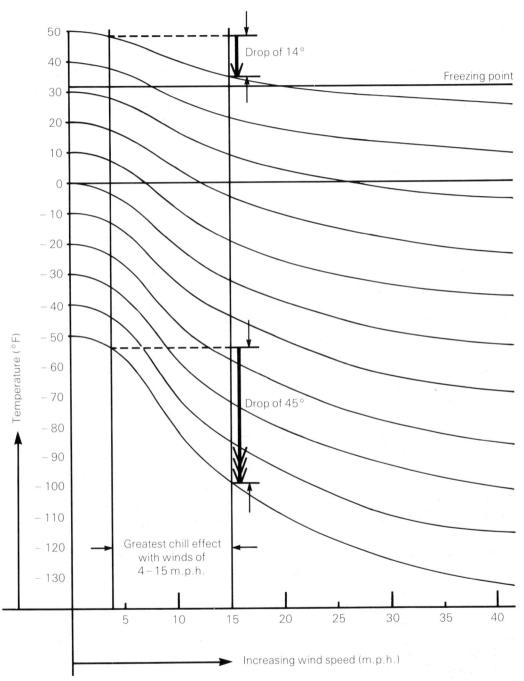

Fig 163   The wind chill effect.

can develop is the most important aspect of prevention. On any trip – even a one-day excursion – where sudden changes in weather can occur, clothing adequate to protect as much exposed skin as possible must be worn or carried. A bivouac sac or poly bag is the most compact, easily carried protection in the event of a forced bivouac.

Alertness to the early symptoms is the key. Early signs may be undue fatigue, weakness, slowness, apathy, forgetfulness, and confusion. These symptoms must not be too readily ascribed to fatigue.

The course of hypothermia may be short. In extreme weather it may strike an inadequately clothed climber within an hour. The interval between the onset of symptoms and collapse may be as short as one hour, and the interval between collapse and death may be only two hours.

When muscular incoordination or mental impairment are evident, hypothermia is already serious. Confused, clumsy hypothermic climbers who cannot use their hands are in big trouble: the game may already have been lost.

A bivouac shelter should provide protection from wind, precipitation, and surface water. Insulation from the ground, snow or ice should be arranged. Don all available clothing. Several folk huddling together conserve heat better than individuals in separate shelters and weaker members can be observed and treated more easily. Even if clothing or sleeping bags gradually become damp or wet they should not be discarded, since the inner layers tend to stay warm and the transfer of body heat to the environment is slowed.

To prevent further heat loss, adequate water and food intake are essential for survival. Since thirst is usually not experienced during dehydration, a conscious effort to consume adequate fluid may be necessary. Hot liquids are best. The eating of snow consumes body heat to warm the resulting liquid to body temperature and is not recommended as a source of fluid.

Food replenishes energy and is essential for continued heat production to maintain body temperature as well as for physical effort. Fruit or fruit drinks, chocolate, salted nuts, and tinned meats should be carried as emergency rations. Eating small amounts of food at frequent intervals helps prevent depletion of body energy during the day.

Treatment

Even after external warming has begun, core body temperature may continue to fall for one or two hours. For this reason, early recognition of the existence of hypothermia, prompt treatment and continuation of that treatment until normal body temperature is restored, are essential.

Wet clothing should be removed and replaced with warm, dry garments. The victim must be warmed. Rewarming cannot be carried out effectively simply by placing the patient in a sleeping bag. A sleeping bag only provides insulation, not heat. A patient with no source of heat is only capable of warming the bag to his own depressed body temperature. Some external source of heat must be supplied. Placing a second person with normal body temperature in the bag to provide warmth by direct body-to-body contact has been found to be one of the most effective methods of rewarming. In some circumstances it may be possible to fill bottles with hot water. Care must be taken not to burn the patient.

Patients in deep hypothermia are often thought to be dead. The heartbeat may be inaudible, pulses may not be palpable, and respiration may appear to have ceased. If in doubt, begin mouth-to-mouth resuscitation along with rewarming.

6 World Ice Climbing Areas

The ice climbing world is a wide one and almost anywhere that enjoys a few weeks of freezing weather or a short season of snow, or both, is likely to sport a snow or ice climb – sometime. What follows is only the roughest or world tours; if you intend to address yourself to any one area for more than a day or two (and it is hoped that you will!) then it will almost certainly be worth investing in a guide book and a map for that area. Moreover, I have, on this brief world tour, dealt with Britain in rather more detail than elsewhere. No excuses – it is simply that that is the place I know best. But ice is ice and snow is snow the whole world around – the Equator to both Poles and all between – and though my own experience favours one small corner of it, my taste for the game is catholic and I love it all: about equally.

THE EUROPEAN ALPS, FRANCE AND NORWAY

I doubt if it's an exaggeration to say that the European Alps have both a greater number and variety of ice climbs than anywhere else on the globe – the best advertised collection at any rate. The most popular area is probably the Mont Blanc Massif, for which Chamonix (France) or Courmayeur (Italy) are the usual bases. But whether you choose the Mont Blanc Massif or the Bernese Oberland, or any one of a dozen other equally fine venues, you can be sure that, armed with the appropriate guide book, you'll be spoilt for choice – whatever your ability, experience or inclination, and summer or winter. The winter Alps abound with frozen waterfalls, too, often no more than a few minutes from the road and varying from easy, low-angled, one-pitch climbs to vertical multi-pitchers of the greatest difficulty.

Such has been the development of water climbing in Europe in recent years that you can bet that any waterfall, frozen, is a climb. One of the very best areas for pure ice climbing is the Cirque de Gavarnie in the French Pyrenees, where there are a dozen superb – and usually vertical – ice-falls of up to 1,500ft (450m).

Other areas where an average winter will always provide good ice-fall climbs are: the Val Grande di Lanzo and Valle di Locano in the Paradiso region of Northern Italy; the 12 miles (20km) worth of ice-falls on the road (RN91) between Grenoble and Briancon, particularly at Huez; and the Vallée de la Romanche between Livet and La Grave (actually in three parts – Vallée du Bourg d'Oisan, La Rampe des Commeres and Combe de Malaval). At Huez, for example, 'you can park your car, do two or three bolt protected pitches, then abseil off in time to drink hot chocolate (for the French) or a beer (for the British) at Auberge des Freaux: just like a day at the crags!' Sounds fun. Other good French areas are at Embrun in the Vallon de Fournel above l'Argentière la Bessée, and at Viallins on the road before l'Argentière in the Vallée de la Fressinière.

But it is Norway that has perhaps the best frozen waterfall climbing in the world. The two best known are Vettifossen and

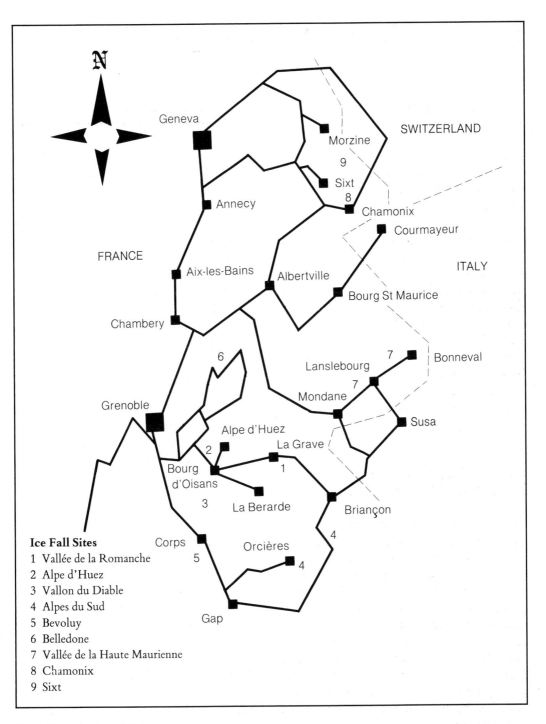

Fig 164   French ice-fall sites.

Ice Fall Sites
1 Vallée de la Romanche
2 Alpe d'Huez
3 Vallon du Diable
4 Alpes du Sud
5 Bevoluy
6 Belledone
7 Vallée de la Haute Maurienne
8 Chamonix
9 Sixt

Mardalsfossen, although there are scores of others the length of Norway – and Norway is 1,500 miles (2,400km) long! (*Fosse* is Norse for waterfall.)

NEW ZEALAND

The Southern Alps of New Zealand are as fine a range of mountains as any that I've climbed in. Mount Cook, 12,349ft (3,764m), is the highest mountain, and Mount Cook village is to its mountain what Chamonix is to Mont Blanc, though on a much smaller commercial scale. Cook itself abounds in great ice climbs – as fine as the rock climbs are lousy. Mount Tasman, too, while Mount Hicks bares a South Face (the Southern hemisphere's equivalent of a Northern hemisphere's North Face) seamed with superb ice routes rather in the Orion Face of Ben Nevis mould, but longer – up to 2,000ft (600m) – and a lot more serious – they're a long way from the road. Other goodies include the South Face of Mount Aspiring and the frozen waterfalls of the Darren Range, south of Cook.

SOUTH AMERICA

The entire length of the Andes between Colombia and Patagonia has much to offer the ice climber. Peru's Cordillera Blanca is the most popular, as well as the most accessible, of the areas, with routes of all grades on anything from porridge to finest water-ice at altitudes between 20,000 and 23,750ft (6,000 and 7,340m). Huaraz is Peru's Chamonix, Third World version, and June and July the best climbing months.

NORTH AMERICA

Alaska

The State of Alaska has Alpine ice and waterfall ice galore. Mount McKinley (Denali), Mount Hunter and Mount Huntington are every bit as fine mountains as their European counterparts, which might be Mont Blanc, the Matterhorn and the Eiger. Some would argue that they are finer, and having climbed one of Alaska's jewels – Mount Deborah – I would hesitate to disagree. The big mountains of Alaska have special problems of weather and access and are not the place for first experiences. For waterfall ice there is Valdez, where in the winter months and only minutes from the road you'll find a hundred ice climbs of all grades. Remember, though, days are short in December and January; February and March will give you more time.

The Lower Forty-nine

As might be expected of so vast an area, the United States owns a wide, and widespread, variety of ice climbing. The North-eastern States have fine winter ice at, amongst a greater selection, Cathedral Ledge in North Conway, New Hampshire, with dozens of superb climbs, of which two of the better known are Repentance and Remission. Frankenstein Cliff, not far away, gives routes of all grades up to 330ft (100m); Cannon Mountain has serious routes up to 660ft (200m), while the gullies of Huntington Ravine (the birthplace of US winter ice climbing back in the 1920s) blow winds that have been measured at over 200 miles (320km) an hour. That's fierce, even by Cairngorm standards!

Vermont, too, has ice climbs, at Lake Willowby. They are fairly hard and perhaps the best is the Promenade, a climb of similar length and difficulty to Colorado's more famous Bridal-Veil Falls. But the best North-eastern ice is to be found north of the US border in Quebec Province (*see* Canada).

There are good summer gullies on the mountains of Wyoming and Montana, of which the best known is the Black Ice Couloir of the Tetons. Both states also sport very good, but little known, winter waterfall climbing. Like anywhere else with water to spare and cold winters, what freezes is ice, and what's ice is climbed.

Colorado and Utah have little, if anything, in the way of Alpine ice, but plenty of winter waterfalls. Some of the best areas are above the road in Provo Canyon, Utah and in the Ouray/Silverton/Telluride area in the San Juan mountains of South-west Colorado, where the Bridal-Veil and Ames Falls are to be found. The Rocky Mountain National Park, around Denver and Boulder, has better mixed than pure ice climbing, with some short, but very hard, routes.

The Sierra Nevada of California contains a number of fine 'autumn' gullies, such as the V-Notch, the U-Notch and the Mendel Couloir. Further north, there are grand mountains with Alpine ice, like Hood; further north still, in Washington, Mount Rainier and the Cascade Mountains offer endless scope for entertainment. Anyone on the look-out for new routes might take a drive along the Colorado Basin, south of the Grand Coulee Dam where, on either side and never very far from the road, are dozens of ice-falls, climbed and unclimbed, up to 500ft (150m) high. With names like Kickaboo Joy Juice, with short, flat, and in some cases downhill approaches, and with the odd telegraph pole to belay to, it's an ice climber's paradise. Or scout around Leanenworth – you'll find plenty of ice and climbs like The Pencil and Drury Falls on the road to Stevens Pass.

Canada

The North American premier ice climbing area is in the Canadian Rockies between Banff and Jasper – these are the Alps of Canada. In summer and autumn here are dozens of couloir/gully and face climbs on Alpine ice. The Columbia Icefields Campground is an especially good area, with terrific ice routes all around from the friendly North Faces of Athabasca and Andromeda, to great ice routes like Slipstream and Grand Central Couloir. Some of the best waterfalls of the world are Canadian: Cascade Falls, Professor's Gully, or, harder, Takkakkaw Falls, Bourgeau Left, or, harder still, the Terminator on Mount Rundle and Gimme Shelter on Mount Quandra – climbs of the best and hardest. There is yet much to be done in the Canadian Rockies, but be warned, it's a cold place in winter, 40–50°F (40–45°C) below, and there's often a high risk of avalanche, a risk prolonged by the consistently low temperatures.

Other areas of Canadian ice include the great massifs of Mount Logan and Mount St Elias with climbing on a McKinley scale, the Coast range and Mount Waddington, 100 miles (160km) north of Vancouver. These are remote and heavily glaciated areas with ice adventures galore for the enterprising – in big country. Easier to get to are the Scottish-type winter climbs on Vancouver Island, on Mount Colonel Foster amongst others.

Over on the East there's Malbaie Valley in

Quebec Province and 1,000ft (300m) plums such as Mont Gros Bras, Cristal V, L'Equerre and La Pomme d'Or.

And there it is: a rapid world tour; a taster; no more than a scraping of snow off the world's ice routes. *Aficionados* of any one of these areas will consider that rather less than justice has been done to their playground. No matter; they can redress their grievance with actions rather than words. Some areas I have omitted altogether: Africa, for instance, which might be considered an unlikely continent for ice climbing, but which none the less holds, in Mount Kenya's Diamond Couloir, one of the great ice climbs of the world; or New Guinea's Carstensz Pyramid, or the Arctic and Antarctic. But then, if you're wandering that far afield, you'll have advanced far beyond the scope of this taster; an early pointer at best.

INTERNATIONAL GRADINGS

Jeff Lowe, a leading American Alpinist and ice climber of the first water, has compiled an interesting and useful 'comparison of ice climbs around the world'. In his section 'Ice Climbing' of a fine book *Climbing* by Ron Fawcett, Jeff Lowe, Paul Nunn and Alan Rouse (Unwin Hyman Ltd; published in North America by Sierra Club Books as *The Climber's Handbook*) he explains:

'In 1979 I introduced a rating system for ice climbing which has been widely adopted in America, and which is designed such that it can be used to describe climbs throughout the world. Basically this system uses a grading that was developed to describe the overall difficulties of rock climbs in Yosemite Valley. Length, continuity, most difficult pitch, seriousness, and commitment are all taken into account in a scale of Roman numerals I to VI, with most grade VI's requiring two or more days and 680m or more of hard climbing, although today's best climbers can often complete such routes in one day. To this six-grade scale, I have added a seventh which is necessary to describe the biggest and hardest Himalayan Alpine-style climbs with their greater size, altitude, and commitment.

In addition to the overall grade, there is another useful rating that describes the hardest technical section of the route, thus helping to differentiate between long climbs of moderate difficulty and short climbs of great technical challenge that may merit the same overall grade.

For the technical rating it is convenient to start with the Scottish grades of 1 to 6, which were originally intended only to convey a sense of overall difficulties similar to the Yosemite rating, but for ice climbs. Over the years, however, the Scottish system has sometimes been misused to describe individual move and pitch difficulties. It is this bastardised use that I have found useful in describing the technical problems that one may expect on a given climb under 'average' conditions. Once again, a seventh grade has been added to the technical scale to accommodate today's hardest mixed climbs. It is useful to designate the type of ice to be found on a climb by the capital letters AI or WI preceding the technical grade, indicating permanent Alpine Ice, or seasonal Winter Ice.'

(*See* Fig 165 for a comparison of ice climbs around the world by Jeff Lowe.)

Overall Grade	North America	Scotland	Alps	New Zealand	Cordillera Blanca	Himalaya
I	Standard Route; Frankenstein Cliff, N H	Comb Gully, Ben Nevis				Kalar Patar
II	Skyladder, Mt Andromeda	Green Gully, Ben Nevis	Standard Route; Mt Blanc du Tacul		Standard Route; on Pisco	
III	Repentance, Cathedral Ledge	Point Five Gully, Ben Nevis	Gervasutti Couloir, Mt Blanc du Tacul	Standard Route; Mt Cook	S. Face, Artesonraju	Standard Route; Island Peak
IV	Black Ice Couloir, Grand Teton	Orion Face Direct, Ben Nevis	N. Face, Triolet	Balfour Face, Mt Tasman	S. Face, Ochshapalca	Standard Route; Lobuje Peak
V	Grand Central Couloir, Mt Kitchener	Vertigo Wall, Cairngorms	N. Face, Le Droit	Hardest Routes; S. Face of Hicks	Bouchard Route; Chacraraju	
VI	Logan/Stump Emperor Face, Mt Robson		1966 Eiger Direct		S.W. Spur, Taulliraju	S. Face Ama Dablam
VII						Hungo Face, Kwangde

Technical Grade	North America	Scotland	Alps	New Zealand	Cordillera Blanca	Himalaya
1	Muir Route; Mt Ranier	Number 3 Gully, Ben Nevis	Standard Route; Mt Blanc du Tacul		Standard Route; Pisco	
2	Skyladder, Mt Andromeda	Number 2 Gully, Ben Nevis	Gervasutti Couloir, Mt Blanc du Tacul		S. Face, Artesonraju	Island Peak
3	Black Ice Couloir, Grand Teton	Comb Gully, Ben Nevis	N. Face, Triolet	Caroline Face, Mt Cook	S.W. Face, Pyramid de Garcilaso	Lobuje Peak
4	Original Route, Glenwood Ice Fall	Green Gully, Ben Nevis	Gabbarrou/Albinoni, Mt Blanc du Tacul			
5	Repentance, Cathedral Ledge	Point Five Gully and Orion Face Direct	Super Couloir, Mt Blanc du Tacul	Balfour Face, Mt Tasman	S. Face, Chacraraju	S. Face, Ama Dablam
6	Bridal-Veil Falls, Colorado	Citadel/Sticil Face, Shelter Stone	Voie de l'Overdose, Gavarnie	Sorenson/Cradock, S. Face Hicks	S. Face, Trapecio	Hungo Face, Kwangde
7	Hot Doggies, Rocky Mountain National Park	The Needle, Shelter Stone				

Fig 165 *A comparative grading of ice climbs around the world.*

Grades of climbs are in brackets after the name, for example Devil's Appendix (5).

GREAT BRITAIN

North Wales

Guide Books: Winter Climbs in North Wales, by Rick Newcombe (Cicerone). *Welsh Winter Climbs*, by Malcolm Campbell and Andy Newton (Cicerone).

Craig yr Ysfa (Carneddau)

Map: OS 1:50,000, sheet 115 (grid reference 693637).
Nearest road: the A5, Capel Curig – Bangor at grid reference 687603. Follow the Water Authority road up the hillside to Ffynnon Llugwy and through a col to the cliff. 2 miles (3.2km), 1,750ft (525m); 1¾ hours.
Campsite/bunkhouses: MAM, CC, LUMC, and Leicester MC huts in Ogwen Valley and Cwm Eigiau. Camping at Gwern y Gof Isaf.

Black Ladders (Carneddau)

Map: OS 1:50,000, sheet 115 (grid reference 670632).
Nearest road: minor road south of Gerlan above Bethesda (grid reference 638659). Through marshy fields to Cwm Llafar and then by a good path to the cliff. 2¼ miles (3.6km), 1,300ft (390m); 1½ hours.
Campsites/bunkhouses: Campsite below the cliff or in the Ogwen Valley. Huts and hostel in the Ogwen Valley.

Cwm Idwal (Glyders)

Map: OS 1:50,000, sheet 115 (grid reference 638589).

Nearest road: A5 Capel Curig – Bangor road at Ogwen Cottage (grid reference 650603). 1 mile (1.6km), 600ft (180m); ¾ hour.
Campsites/bunkhouses: as for Craig yr Ysfa, plus Idwal Cottage Youth Hostel or camping in Cwm Idwal.

Snowdon Summit, Lliwedd and Llanberis Pass

Map: OS 1:50,000, sheet 115.
Nearest road: A4086 Capel Curig – Llanberis. North face of Lliwedd, 2 miles (3.2km), 1,100ft (330m); 2 hours. Snowdon Summit Gullies, 2½ miles (4km), 2,000ft (600m); 2 hours. Craig y Rhaeadr – Llanberis Pass, 1 mile (1.6km), 1,000ft (300m); 40 minutes. In a hard winter there are a dozen gullies and frozen water-weeps on either side of the pass varying in grade from 1 to 5 and in approach time from 10 minutes to 1 hour.
Campsite/bunkhouse: campsite at the farm and at Ynnes Ettws CC hut. Youth Hostel at Pen y Pass (grid reference 647556).

Good Routes

Craig yr Ysfa: Great Gully (3/4).
Black Ladders: Western Gully (4), Eastern Gully (2), Pyramid Gully (4).
Cwm Idwal: Devil's Appendix (5), South Gully (3/4), Chicane Gully (2/3), Devil's Staircase (4), Central Gully (3), Clogwyn Du Gully (left-hand branch) (4).
Lliwedd: Central Gully (4), Slanting Gully (4).
Craig y Rhaeadr: Cascade (4), Central Ice Fall Direct (5), Waterfall Climb (3).
The Snowdon Summit Gullies: Left-hand Trinity (1), Central Trinity (1), Right-hand Trinity (2), Trinity Buttress (3), Ladies

Gully (3), Snowdrop (4).
Clogwyn du'r Arddu: Black Cleft (6).
Cader Idris: Trojan (4), The Great Gully (2).

Gully (3).
Comb Gill: Raven Crag Gully (3), (grid reference 248114).

The Lake District

Guide Book: Winter Climbs in The Lake District, R. Bennett, W. Birkett and A. Hyslop (Cicerone).

Scotland

Note: only the five most frequented areas are included, which leaves some notable omissions.

Great End (Scafell Group)

Map: OS 1:63,360 Tourist Map – Lake District (grid reference 228085).
Nearest road: a minor road at Seathwaite (grid reference 236122), at the end of Borrowdale. 3 miles (4.8km), 2,000ft (600m); 2 hours.
Campsites/bunkhouses: campsites in Langdale, Borrowdale, Wasdale. Solving House (FRCC) in Rosthwaite. Other FRCC huts in Langdale and Wasdale.

Scafell Crag

Map: OS 1:63,360 Tourist Map – Lake District (grid reference 205069).
Nearest road: Wasdale Head campsite (grid reference 181076). 2 miles (3.2km), 2,200ft (660m); 2 hours.
Campsites/bunkhouses: National Trust campsite at Wasdale Head. Bracken Close (grid reference 184073) is the nearest climbing hut (FRCC). Bunkhouse at the Wastwater Hotel.

Good Routes

Scafell Crag: Moss Ghyll (4), Steep Ghyll (4/5).
Falcon Crag: Helvellyn (grid reference 352126) Chock Gully (3/4).
Great End: South East Gully (2/3), Central

Guide Books: SMC Rock and Ice Climbs in Lochaber and Badenoch, by A. C. Stead and J. R. Marshall. *Scottish Winter Climbs*, by Hamish MacInnes (Constable). *Winter Climbs – Ben Nevis and Glencoe*, by Ed Grindlay (Cicerone).
Map: OS 1:50,000, sheet 41.
Nearest road: A82 Fort William–Spean Bridge at a lay-by (grid reference 137763) or the golf course car park. A path leads across the golf course to a stile, then up a steep, muddy, wooded hillside to a second stile and the Allt a Mhuillin, and thence to the CIC hut: 3½ miles (5.6km), 2,800ft (840m); up to 3 hours. This approach can be halved if you drive up to the Allt a Mhuillin stile by a rough forestry track. Permission to do this should be sought from the Forestry Office at Torlundy on the A82 (grid reference 143771).
Campsites/bunkhouses: CIC hut (SMC), Steall hut (JMCS) Glen Nevis; very early booking essential for both. Youth Hostel in Glen Nevis. Camping in Glen Nevis and anywhere along the Allt a Mhuillin – and even above the CIC hut.
Some good routes: Ben Nevis has more good routes than any other area of Britain. A smattering are: Castle Ridge (2), Tower Ridge (3), North East Buttress (3/4), Comb Gully (3/4), Green Gully (5), Tower Scoop

(3), Italian Climb (3), Glovers Chimney (3/4), Ledge Route (1), Curtain (4), Gardyloo Gully (2/3), Orion Face Direct (5), Minus Two Gully (5), Observatory Ridge (3), Smiths Route on Gardyloo Buttress (5), Route 2 (5).

Note: descents are tricky in poor visibility and should be thoroughly researched.

Glencoe

Guide Books: Glencoe and Glen Etive, by Ken Crockett. *Winter Climbs – Ben Nevis and Glencoe,* by Ed Grindlay (Cicerone). *Scottish Winter Climbs,* by Hamish MacInnes (Constable).
Map: OS 1:50,000, sheet 41.
Nearest road: A82 Crianlarich–Glencoe. Approaches to Buachaille Etive Mor from Altnafeadh (grid reference 221563): 1 mile (1.6km), 600ft (180m); 1 hour. To Stob Coire nan Lochan from the Meeting of Three Waters (grid reference 175567): 1 mile (1.6km), 2,000ft (600m); 2 hours. To Aonach Dubh (West Face) from the road junction at the end of Loch Achtriochton (grid reference 138567): 2 miles (3.2km), 1,200ft (360m); 1 hour. To Stob Coire nam Beith from the road junction at the end of Loch Achtriochtan: 1½ miles (2.4km), 2,000ft (600m); 1½ hours.
Campsites/bunkhouses: SMC Lagangarloh; Creag Dhu Hut, Jacksonville; LSCC Hut, Blackrock Cottage, Grampian Club Hut, Glen Etive, Glencoe Youth Hostel, Macall's Bunkhouse, Clachaig Inn; campsites at the King's House; Glencoe and upper Glen Etive.
Good routes: on Buachaille Etive Mor are Crowberry Gully (3), Curved Ridge (1/2), Raven's Gully (5), Crowberry Ridge (3). On Stob Coire nan Lochan are SC Gully (3) and Twisting Gully (2/3). On Aonach

Dubh (west face) are No.6 Gully (3), No.5 Gully (3), The Screen (3/4), CD Scoop (3) and Chaos Chimney (3). On Stob Coire nam Beith are Deep Cut Chimney (3/4), Central Gully (3) and North-west Gully (2/3).

Across the road the Aonach Eagach Ridge provides one of the best scrambles in Great Britain at Grade 1. Another gem is Sron Na Lairig Ridge (1/2), tucked away behind Buachaille Etive Beag (grid reference 157535).

Creag Meagaidh

Guide Books: SMC Guide to Rock and Ice Climbs in *Lochaber and Badenoch* by A.C. Stead and J.R. Marshall; *Winter Climbs – Cairngorms* by John Cunningham and Allen Fyffe (Cicerone); *Scottish Winter Climbs* by Hamish MacInnes (Constable).
Map: OS 1:50,000, sheet 34.
Nearest road: A86 Spean Bridge-Newtonmore at Aberarder Farm (grid reference 483875): 4 miles, 1,300ft (390m); 2½ hours.
Campsites/bunkhouses: camping sometimes possible at Aberarder Farm; camp areas in Coire Ardair; bunkhouse at Fersit, west of Loch Laggan.
Good routes: Staghorn Gully (3), Ritchie's Gully (3/4), Smith's Gully (5), Eastern Corner (3), Northpost (5), Southpost (3), Southpost Direct (5), Pumpkin (4/5), The Sash (2/3).

Note: descents are tricky in poor visibility.

Cairngorms

Guide Books: SMC *Cairngorms,* volumes I–V. *Winter Climbs – Cairngorms* by John Cunningham and Allen Fyffe (Cicerone). *Scottish Winter Climbs* by Hamish MacInnes (Constable).

Maps: OS 1:50,000, sheet 36.

Nearest road: for the northern Cairngorms, the Coire Cas car park, 9 miles (14.4km) south-east of Aviemore (grid reference 990059).

Approaches: to the Northern Corries, Coire an Lochan (grid reference 986028): 3 miles (4.8km), 1,300ft (390m); 1½ hours. To Coire ant-Sneachda (grid reference 993031): 2 miles (3.2km), 1,300ft (390m); 1 hour. Shelter Stone Crag (grid reference 005014) 2½ miles (4km) from the top of the chair-lift, 1½ hours downhill. For Cairn Etchachan (grid reference 009016) the approach is as for Shelter Stone Crag.

Campsites/bunkhouses: Youth Hostels at Aviemore and Loch Morlich; camping at Glenmore campsite; shelter at Hutchison Memorial Hut in Coire Etchachan (grid reference 023997) and bivouac at the Shelter Stone (grid reference 001016).

Good routes: In the Northern Corries there are a dozen good, short, fairly easy climbs to choose from. On Hell's Lum Crag are Deep-cut Chimney (3/4), The Chancer (4), Hell's Lum Chimney (2/3) and Devil's Delight (5). On Shelter Stone Crag are Sticil Face (5), Castle Wall (3) and Pinnacle Gully (1).

On Cairn Etchachan are Scorpion (5), Route Major (4) and Castlegates Gully (1).

Lochnagar

Guide Books: SMC *Cairngorms* volumes IV and V by G.S. Strange and D.S. Dinwoodie. *Scottish Winter Climbs* by Hamish MacInnes (Constable). *Winter Climbs – Cairngorms* by J. Cunningham and A. Fyffe (Cicerone).

Map: OS 1:50,000, sheet 44 (grid reference 253857).

Nearest road: a car park at the Spittal of Glen Muick (grid reference 310851) at the end of a minor road 9 miles (14.4km) south-west of Ballater: 4½ miles (7.2km), 1,800ft (540m); 2½ hours.

Campsites/bunkhouses: discrete camping is possible in Glen Muick; Aberdeen University Hut at Allt-na-Guibhsaich (grid reference 298858).

Good routes: Tough Brown Traverse (3), Polyphemus Gully (4), Parallel Gully B (5), Raeburns Gully (2), Pinnacle Face (5), Eagle Ridge (5), Parallel Gully A (3), Pinnacle Gully I (2), Pinnacle Gully II (2), Black Spout Buttress (3), Black Spout (1).

Appendix

These two tales first appeared in *Cold Climbs* (*see* Further Reading). The first climb is at Raven's Gully (500ft/150m, Grade 5), Buachaille Etive Mor, Glencoe; the second, the Devil's Appendix (300ft/90m, Grade 5), Cwm Idwal, Snowdonia.

RAVEN'S WITH THE GREAT MAN

We parked by Altnafeadh and bundled out, six of us, in a welter of gear. Then the boot door was hoisted skywards, triggering an avalanche of equipment. The accoutrements of modern ice are awesome. I watched the great man with interest – and some nervousness. After all, here in our very midst was one of the glitterati, the embodiment of *jeunesse dorée* and BMC National Officer to boot. We would watch and learn. I knew little about the man except that he had climbed Everest and was reputed to be a nice bloke.

The five of us waited, respectfully allowing Pete first shot at the mountain of gear that lay strewn half-way across the A82. If we expected him to gird himself crisply like some latter-day gladiator, as I think we did, we were to be cruelly disappointed. Indeed, he paraded woefully ill-equipped, lack-lustre even, standing before us sporting not much more than odd stockings, two very pedestrian axes and a supreme indifference to the arsenal which lay all about.

'Don't forget the ropes,' he said, and set off towards Great Gully, a painfully thin sack flapping in the wind.

That wind! It was a wild day even down here and Raven's did not look friendly. See it for yourself on one of those raw Rannoch days and you will assuredly agree. This is the Buachaille's bad side; black, malevolent, and the slit of Raven's blacker still. Not friendly. No flirt here with a fine lace of chantilly ice, nor any smile of firmly compliant, sparkling névé beckoning to a summit altar. No, sir. Black walls and a black-eyed gully, trapped in a bleak embrace between Slime Wall (what horrors that name conjures for the PA-shod) and Cuneiform Buttress. Hobson's choice.

Then the wind did for two of them. The wind and an escape ploy that would have graced Patey's pages.

'I live here,' protested Allan, 'I can afford to wait for better weather. Do it any time.' His partner quickly clipped into the same gambit and they turned with the wind and ran goose-winged back to the car. I envied their sanity, admired their courage, looked askance at Pete. The great man, his face set in an expression of frozen insouciance, resolutely plodded on, lugubrious to the last but betraying no sign of the hangover that should have been beheading him.

In an hour we gathered at the foot of a gully of steep, soft snow that drowned the first three (summer) pitches and led straight to a chockstone roof which forms the summer crux. Pete surged forward. If I half expected a Red Sea parting of the powder to allow him unimpeded passage, I was, for a second time, disenchanted. The great man flailed, grunted and swam – the last a badly co-ordinated butterfly stroke – in a distinctly mortal fashion, to collapse in a terrible wrack of panting just below the chockstone. We three followed easily up a well-bulldozed trough. Here Martin Burrows Smith, who instructs these things, suggested that it might be a good thing to rope up. He joined with Pete, I with Paul Moores.

Pete, now recovered, went at the crux, the wall to the left of the chockstone. It spat him back. Obviously there was even more to Raven's than met the eye.

'My dad did this in 1945 in army boots,' I observed, trying to sound helpful. Whether Pete believed me (and it's true) I have never discovered, but it goaded him to a fury, galvanised him. He charged full frontal to the breach and squeezed up the full 5a of it, axes and crampons sparking where his bludgeon laid bare the rock. The rope ran out at an alarming rate.

I followed, leading my half of the team. It was hard. Jams for the right arm and foot, left axe anxiously searching skyhook in-cuts. Left front-points despairing a lack of ice, and crampons complaining cacophonous on bare rock. Just when I thought I might be off – downwards – a careless knot in Pete's rope caught between my left front-points and lent me that tiny tug which measures the mile between up and down. Such was the great man's surge up the easy slope beyond that he was unaware of his 12-stone parasite.

I joined him at the mouth of the cave below a second enormous chockstone. It was wilder here. As wild as Smith or Marshall could have ever asked for. Wilder than we wanted, 'wild above rule or art'. The moor had been rough, but this was something else. A vortex of omnidirectional, supersonic spindrift that numbed the senses and stung the flesh. Straight to the

vein like the Stones' chords or Sibelius' crescendos – go to Raven's on a wild day and you will feel what I mean.

The four of us crawled deeper into the cave and found an eerie haven. Martin produced a flask of coffee, Paul a great nugget of chocolate, I a packet of biscuits. Pete, without so much as a 'by your leave', tucked into all three simultaneously.

'The sports plan is this,' he said at length in superstar-speak, 'there are three or four gigantic chockstones at intervals above this one. With luck they'll all provide a cave just like this. One of you will lead and fix the rope so the rest of us can use it to save time. I've already done the crux for you, so you should be OK now. Anyway, I'm a greater-ranges man myself.' Sips of coffee then,

'Now, you go first Paul.'

Paul steeled himself and crawled back to the maelstrom. He had not gone ten feet before we lost sight and sound of him, but thirty seconds later he was back, gasping like a pearl diver.

'What's the problem?' asked Pete, into a mug of coffee.

'Can't breathe out there, or see a thing either.'

'Take a deep breath and just keep going upwards – the line's obvious,' advised Pete through a biscuit. 'And give the rope a couple of tugs when you want us to come up.'

Poor old Paul. He huffed and he puffed and he puffed and he huffed; and he hyperventilated. Then over the top. Pete kicked a dozen coils towards the entrance.

'Enough for him to be going on with.' The minutes ticked by as we chatted comfortably over our coffee and biscuits. From time to time one of us, following the great man's example, would foot a few yards of rope to the void, scuttling quickly back to the sanctuary.

'Much like this on the summit push on the Big E,' Pete observed casually, adding with equal nonchalance, '28,000ft higher on Big E, of course'. Difficult to follow that, and though I struggled for a riposte none came within 20,000ft.

At last the rope went tight and two tugs signalled an end to our coffee break. Out we went, Somme-style. The weather was daunting; this surely was Armageddon. The wind tore at you, tore into you, snatched the breath from between your teeth before you'd barely tasted it, buffeted the brain insensate and knocked at the heart, challenging 'climb me if you dare'. And where or what are you? What pleasures are the draught of this moment? To be sure there's no space, no freedom, no grace or joy in movement. The world ends three inches in front of your face, limbs go where they can, where they will stay, and you seldom see where that is. Can this be the same game that we play in the sun on those slabs a few miles away around the corner? That gambol in shorts with chalk and rubbers. The one a series of deliberate moves, like physical arithmetic; the other a blind, wanton struggle – a gravitational gamble. Can this be the same game? The brain says 'No, not at all!', but the soul shouts to be heard: 'Yes it is!'

Martin's turn. Out he goes. Out come the coffee and biscuits. And so we went on. When my turn came I struggled upwards for twenty minutes with little idea where I was until I found myself in the lee of an enormous chasm, 100ft deep. I cast about, looking for the gully continuation which refused to reveal itself, fixed the ropes and tugged. The others quickly joined me, Pete looking greatly exercised:

'This is the Direct Finish,' he said,

'Chouinard did it. Chimneyed it, and he's even shorter than you.' I didn't believe him. Still don't.

'Got to do something for the second half of your pitch.' The comment chided me down and across left to where I found the groove of the original finish. The climbing was steady, pegs here and there and an occasional glimpse over the left shoulder through the storm to Slime Wall and an evil-looking Shibboleth. A winter ascent of that lot? I hugged at my groove and fought back the images that shivered involuntarily across the inward eye, sowing a seed in the subconscious. It lingers yet, barren, I hope.

There's a landing 15ft from the top, where we joined, then a convoluted corkscrew of a problem pitch and it's all over. We were out. Out of the vortex, gone from the maelstrom, with nothing worse than the screech of the wind and a scoot down Great Gully to worry us.

The great man spoke and I waited for a leg-pull:

'That's the best day on the hill I've ever had.' His face creased with pleasure and four huge smiles exploded far wider than that Direct Finish. Raven's had beaten *badinage*.

Postscript

I wrote this on the bus coming back from Chamonix. A few minutes after I had put down that last full stop we pulled into Victoria where I bought a newspaper. Peter Boardman, it told me, was dead on Everest. Stricken, I returned to this story and hacked at all that now seemed in bad taste; daft, of course, but understandable I hope. Most of it is back now, as it should be, as he would have asked.

The sad thing is that he had wanted to write about Raven's for *Cold Climbs*. It was his best day on the hill, he repeated. I refused to budge for reasons I can scarcely admit even to myself. If only I had.

I wish that this were a story of enough merit to match Pete's best day, a best story for his best day. Alas, the gift is not mine to give, but it was a great day, on a fine climb, with a great mate – and a marvellous memory.

DEVIL'S APPENDIX

To the Unknown Climber

There was a queue. It was, I suppose, to be expected, for seldom does the Devil bare his Appendix. Boysen was impatient. He nearly always is. We were fourth or fifth in line, which wasn't anything like good enough for him. Wasn't it sufficient frustration that the first ascent should have been snatched by two unknown upstarts without so much as a credential between them, whilst he, doyen and co-creator of the Black Cleft and a dozen other Welsh winter horrors, hungered impotently in Altrincham?

The year before, Joe Brown had stood second in the queue while those upstarts stole the route from under his nose. Joe's partner was Davey Jones of Ogwen Cottage, and although the Appendix grew like Jack's beanstalk out of his backyard, they were still beaten to it. It was a terrible thing. Mind you, as the upstarts would doubtless be the first to point out, folk, including Small Brown, had been sniffing at it for fifteen years, dogs round the Devil's Lamp-post. And for fifteen years the 'out of condition' ploy had conceded defeat to the physical and psychological barrier of 300ft of very steep ice. How strange, then, that the route has been in peak condition for three or

four years since that first ascent. A new ice-age, or new ice-tools. . . ? Full marks to the upstarts.

After its fifteen years of growing into climbers' consciousness, the Appendix aged rapidly. First climbed by two unknown Englishmen; second ascent three minutes later by an indigenous instructor and an ageing rock star. Shortly afterwards a Scot declared that his country had nothing like it, which is as close as those north of the border will come to admitting that they found a climb south of it hard. In 1981 an Irishman soloed it for Christmas.

Martin stomped about, all sulphurous vim and vigour, for two minutes or so, before exhausting what passed in him for patience and charging off to find another route. I followed reluctantly in his wake. After all, it was a grand day, and a couple of hours of Appendix-watching suited me fine. I lived just down the road and could nip up in a minute on any of the next two or three times this century that the Devil obliged us with his route. But Martin, fraught from the teaching of biology to fifteen-year-old recalcitrants, needed his climb and needed it quick.

He selected an improbable line and shot up it to snatch the first winter ascent of the Devil's Pipes. Ten minutes later we were back at the foot of the Appendix, where the queue was scarcely diminished, although a man and wife team were abseiling off the climb. While she froze at her belay, he had struggled manfully to the top of the first pitch, at which point, extended beyond the call of marital duty and his own ability, he abseiled off, muttering that it was 'too hard for the wife'. Surely the most unchivalrous 'climbing down gracefully' ploy of all time.

Martin set about the rest of the queue with the same galvanic energy with which he had cleared out the Pipes. I could but wonder at his nerve. Aspirants five and six were despatched to a 'much better route' around the corner. Lamely they departed, only, as I later discovered, to fail on this improvement. Numbers three and four were plainly told that the route was far too hard for them and, relieved of their burden, they wandered happily away in search of easier ground. One and two, made of sterner stuff, held their ground and prepared to launch themselves at the first pitch, with Martin, outraged at this intrusion into the Master's design, castigating their temerity. I marvelled at the hauteur of the great.

Even as I marvelled, a second energy registered somewhere in the subconscious. The atmosphere was suddenly gravid with matters of great moment. As though drawn by some psychic power (or, on reflection, it might have been those awful animal grunts) our heads were turned as one, our gaze riveted by an unforgettable display.

Just across the 'Kitchen' an instructor front-pointed with fastidious precision to the upper rim of an ice cliff, where he paused, *Piolet Gibbon*, in order to demonstrate some arcanum to assembled and awestruck tiros. Extracting his dues in gasps of admiration, he disappeared from his charges' view and pounded up the ensuing 40-degree snow slope in search of a belay. He was 150ft from the ground, but still 10ft short of his target, when the first victim, assuming a tight rope signalled his turn, set off with prodigal energy.

The pupil flailed upward for 15ft or so, *Piolet Attila*, discovering in those luminous seconds that ice climbing was more biceps than brains. Meanwhile, the instructor sedulously embraced a boulder with a textbook belay, consuming the rope, as chance would have it, at precisely the same speed as the victim climbed. Awesome though the latter's energy was, it was also human, and at 30ft his quadrupedal threshings wilted fast until crampons and axes, lacking power or accuracy, ricocheted to nowhere. Weaker still he grew. A search in the engine room of his soul found a final calorie which fired some terrible grunts and a last convulsion; and then that calorie was thrown, with his axe, to the wind. With no more to give, not even the energy to fuel a yell, he sank into his harness, slumped into the rope, hung free and limp and dangled, as if from a yardarm, 30ft from the ground – utterly spent. Boysen, numbers one, two, and I stood in mute admiration, too stunned to salute. Had I been alone I think I might have wept.

A split second later this stunned silence was shattered. The instructor, having double-checked his belay, squared his gear, fixed feet firmly, checked it all again and found no fault, sat smugly and called with the measured, practised sonority which is the hallmark of those who ply that trade:

'Come up when you are ready.' The command, for such it was, reverberated about the cwm and one by one, separated only by the speed of sound, a dozen spectating teams collapsed in mass hysteria.

Martin pitched forward, face into the snow, clutching at his throat and convulsed in apoplectic laughter. The other Appendix team did much the same while hoots and howls floated up from all around. The whole Kitchen was aboil with laughter.

At last numbers one and two tumbled off, no longer capable of mustering the necessary aggression for an appendectomy; which left Martin and me. One of the departing climbers offered me a shot with a pair of Hummingbird axes:

'Perfect for steep water-ice,' he said. I had never seen them before but thought to give them a try and left my own axes on the floor. Looking up, the flesh of the Appendix was plain to see. A trunk of water-ice rose 120ft to a ledge and belay. At mid-height there was a painful looking swelling, then a comparatively benign groove led up and left for a second 120ft or so. The belay was not obvious. On pitch 3 a horizontal traverse sneaked rightwards to an angry, vertical chunk festooned with malignant icicles, each a huge anti-climber missile as long as a lance. The full breadth of the upper face was hung with these, often grotesquely contorted like the grasping fingers of Hokusai's waves. Some Appendix! I briefly pictured myself picking a way through such a canvas, but here at base imagery escaped me and levity ruled.

I giggled my way up 10ft of steepish ice, where I attempted to lodge a Hummingbird in a vee formed by two converging icicles. They would have accommodated my own axes happily, but for some reason rejected this newfangled tool. As I fiddled, an enormous tug on the rope plucked at me, and glancing quickly down I saw my second pulling on the rope with truly satanic fury. With a levity shattering splat I landed at his feet, where the Hummingbirds were snatched from my wrists. Martin was angry again, cursing my time-wasting, ordering me to use my own gear and get a move on.

I did as I was commanded, fearing Martin more than the Devil – they seemed to be sharing the same pair of horns. Ten minutes later I belayed above 100ft of steep ice. I recall nothing of that first pitch. Martin sprinted up the next and spent all of twenty seconds engineering the worst belay imaginable – an axe loosely jammed across a groove of rotten ice. Faith and his left hand held it in position while he managed the rope with the right.

'Quickly!' he snapped, as I eyed it.

Quickly I went, to the traverse, exposed, exhilarating and 300 near-vertical feet above the floor. And then the final bulge, as exciting as any chunk of ice I can remember.

Not so much to tell about a great ice climb, you will say. Not much indeed, for, though it is a great climb, I still remember the laugh we had better. Anyway, what can you say about steep water-ice? If the axes stay, so do you. And they did; biceps not brains, you see? On the way down the lines of a song occurred to me:

'Now I ain't saying we beat the devil,' but we laughed at his joke for nothing – and then we climbed his climb.

Useful Addresses

GREAT BRITAIN

Association of British Mountain Guides
Private guiding and instruction. Contact through BMC.

British Mountaineering Council (BMC)
Crawford House
Precinct Centre
Booth Street East
Manchester M13 9RZ

Courses, publications, access, insurance, etc. This is the best single source of information and addresses.

Glenmore Lodge
National Outdoor Training Centre
Aviemore
Inverness-shire PH22 1QU

Runs courses on snow and ice climbing.

Mountaineering Council of Scotland
15 Dowiesmill Lane
Edinburgh EH4 6DW

Plas y Brenin
National Centre for Mountain Activities
Capel Curig
Betws y Coed
Gwynedd LL24 0ET

Runs courses on snow and ice climbing.

NORTH AMERICA

American Alpine Club
113 E 90th Street
New York 10128
USA

Alpine Club of Canada
Box 1026
Banff
Alberta
Canada

NEW ZEALAND

Alpine Guides Ltd
Mt Cook
New Zealand

Outdoor Pursuits Centre
Tawhiti Kuri
Private Bag
Turangi
New Zealand

Further Reading

All American books are available in Great Britain through Cordee Books, 3a De Montfort Street, Leicester LE1 7HD; all British books are distributed in North America by Alpenbooks, Snohomish, Washington.

PERIODICAL PUBLICATIONS

Climber: Ravenseft House, 302–304 St Vincent Street, Glasgow.
High: Springfield House, The Parade, Oadby, Leicester.
Mountain: PO Box 184, Sheffield.
Scottish Mountaineering Club Journal: 369 High Street, Edinburgh.
Climbing: PO Box E, Aspen, Colorado 81611, USA.
Rock and Ice: Eldorado Publishing Inc., PO Box 3595, Boulder, Colorado 80307, USA.

American and Canadian Alpine journals are published by their respective clubs (*see* Useful Addresses)

HANDBOOKS

Barry, J. and Jepson, T. *Safety on Mountains* (BMC)
Barton, B. and Wright, B. *A Chance in a Million: Scottish Avalanches* (Scottish Mountaineering Trust)
Blackshaw, A. *Mountaineering* (Kaye and Ward)

Chouinard, Y. *Climbing Ice* (Hodder & Stoughton); published in the USA by Sierra Club Books
Cliffe, P. *Mountain Navigation* (distributed by Cordee)
Daffern, T. *Avalanche Safety for Skiers and Climbers* (Alpenbooks, Snohomish, Washington)
Fawcett, Lowe, Nunn, Rouse, *Climbing* (Unwin Hyman Ltd; published in the USA by Sierra Club Books as *The Climber's Handbook*
Frazer, C. *Avalanches and Snow Safety* (The Chaucer Press)
La Chapelle, E.R. *The ABC of Avalanche Safety* (The Mountaineers, Seattle, Washington)
Langmuir, E. *Mountaincraft and Leadership* (Scottish Sports Council/Mountain Leadership Training Board)
March, W. *Modern Snow and Ice Techniques* (Cicerone Press)
Mitchell, *Mountaineering First Aid*; third edition by Lentz, M., Carline, J. and Macdonald, S. (The Mountaineers, Seattle, Washington)
Rebuffat, G. *On Snow and Rock* (Nicholas Kaye Ltd)
Wilkerson, J.A. *Medicine for Mountaineering* (The Mountaineers, Seattle, Washington)
Hypothermia, Frostbite and Other Cold Injuries: Prevention, Recognition and Prehospital Treatment (The Mountaineers, Seattle, Washington)

GUIDE BOOKS AND GENERAL READING

Barry, J., Wilson, K. and Alcock, D. *Cold Climbs* (Diadem Books)

Bennett, B. and Birkett, B. *Winter Climbs in the Lake District* (Cicerone)

Campbell, M. and Newton, A. *Welsh Winter Climbs* (Cicerone)

Grindley, E. *Winter Climbs – Ben Nevis and Glencoe* (Cicerone)

MacInnes, H. *Scottish Winter Climbs* (Constable)

Nesbitt, A. and Fyffe, A. *Winter Climbs – Cairngorms* (Cicerone)

Newcombe, R. *Winter Climbs in North Wales* (Cicerone)

Scottish Mountaineering Council Rock and Ice Guides to:
Glencoe and Etive
Lochaber and Badenoch
Cuillin of Skye
Cairngorms, volumes I–V
Northern Highlands

North American guide books are beginning to appear and new ones come out regularly. The best approach is to contact the following for the latest selection: Backcountry Bookstore, PO Box 191, Snohomish, Washington 98290, USA.

Index